Most Likely to Succeed

to Succeed

Mark Rutland
with Travis Rutland

Charisma
HOUSE
A Strang Company

Most Strang Communications/Charisma House/Siloam/FrontLine/Excel Books/Realms products are available at special quantity discounts for bulk purchase for sales promotions, premiums, fundraising, and educational needs. For details, write Strang Communications/Charisma House/Siloam/FrontLine/Excel Books/Realms, 600 Rinehart Road, Lake Mary, Florida 32746, or telephone (407) 333-0600.

Most Likely to Succeed
by Mark Rutland with Travis Rutland
Published by Charisma House
A Strang Company
600 Rinehart Road
Lake Mary, Florida 32746
www.charismahouse.com

Cover Designer: studiogearbox.com
Executive Design Director: Bill Johnson

Library of Congress Cataloging-in-Publication Data

Rutland, Mark.
   Most likely to succeed / Mark Rutland with Travis Rutland.
      p. cm.
   Includes bibliographical references.
   ISBN 978-1-59979-251-4
   1.   Success--Religious aspects--Christianity. 2.   High school graduates. 3.   College graduates.   I. Rutland, Travis. II. Title.
   BV4598.3.R88 2008
   248.4--dc22

   2007037937

08 09 10 11 12 — 9 8 7 6 5 4 3 2 1
Printed in the United States of America

Acknowledgments

⟨⟨⟨⟨⟩

I WISH TO ACKNOWLEDGE WITH GRATITUDE THE vital contribution of my son, Travis Rutland. Without his capable and creative editorial work this book would not have been possible. It is humbling to find yourself impressed by your children, yet I am awestruck by all my children. In this work, as in all he undertakes, Travis was insightful, diligent, detail oriented, and able to keep the vision of the work clear. "This is my son, my only son, in whom I am well pleased."

CONTENTS

I

CHARACTER— THE KEYS OF SUCCESS

A man's character is his fate.

—Heraclitus

FIND AN OLD YEARBOOK, YOUR PARENTS' perhaps. Don't the clothes look funny? How about the hairdos? They look quaint and old-timey to you, but they were cool back then, way cool.

What is hard to imagine is that someday your kids, or wilder still, your grandkids, will giggle their way through your yearbook. They will shriek in laughter at your funny clothes and howl at your weird hair.

"Did you wear that?"

"Tell me you didn't really go out of the house like that!"

You think they won't. You are thinking, "My style will never go out of style." But I am here to tell you that all the things that are so now, fifty years from now will be so then that your grandchildren will find them hysterical.

Now turn back to that same old yearbook of your parents. Find the "Senior Superlatives" or whatever they call the page with all those "Bests" and "Mosts."

> THERE ARE SOME KEYS TO SUCCESSFUL LIVING THAT ARE AVAILABLE TO YOU, WHOEVER YOU ARE, IF YOU JUST KNOW WHERE TO FIND THEM.

"Best Looking." Best looking? Are they to you?

"Class Clown." Can you see it? Do they look funny to you?

"Most Athletic." Could they even make the teams at your school?

Now find "Most Likely to Succeed."

Look at them. Look deeply. Look into their hopeful eyes. Study their eager, young faces. What made their classmates select them? Their grades? Maybe. Popularity? That's more likely.

The real question is, did they succeed? Did they really succeed? Did they make lots of money only to ruin their lives? Did they find only empty, shattered relationships?

Or were they successful in all of life? Maybe they succeeded in business or politics or science; maybe they even made a fortune or became leaders in their field while living healthy, balanced lives that enriched others as well as themselves.

What made the difference? What makes a person "Most Likely to Succeed?"

Of course, there are many variables that determine certain outcomes. Talents, skills, and education all play a part in some parts of life.

Yet there are some keys to successful living that are available to you, whoever you are, if you just know where to find them. OK, there may be people in your graduating class with a higher IQ, for whatever that is worth. Some may get the opportunity to attend a more famous college. But those things have little to do with true success. When you come to the end of your life and career, when you sit down with your grandkids for a good chuckle at the old yearbook, how will you look back on your life? You can look back on a life to be proud of. Here are nine keys to make you likely to succeed. I offer them to you because you were not born to be a failure. You were born for success. Take these nine keys in your hand and go for it. There is a reason you were born *you*. Use these keys. Unlock all the doors you come to. Success awaits you. Congratulations; you are about to become "Most Likely to Succeed."

II

COURAGE—THE KEY TO THE KEYS OF SUCCESS

Courage is the ladder on which
all the other virtues mount.

—Clara Booth Luce

The Bradley armored vehicle inched its way onto the bridge. Three soldiers, Americans, young and with everything to live for, crouched low as they followed, their eyes on the old woman. Bullets from the Iraqi guns on the far side of the river bounced off the sides of the vehicle and the steel girders of the bridge. The soldiers kept coming, risking their lives with every step, braving the enemy guns, all for the life of the elderly Iraqi woman huddled in the gun smoke.

The officer in charge tossed a smoke grenade, and three Americans ran forward to pull the woman to safety. Captain Chris Carter, at the ripe old age of thirty-one, was the company commander. He ordered his men to retreat, carrying the woman, while he gave covering fire with an M-16.

On March 31, 2003, Captain Chris Carter and his men acted courageously on a bridge somewhere south of Baghdad. They were not merely brave but courageous, risking their lives for a defenseless woman in danger from the bullets of her nation's army.[1]

The first and most important key to successful living is courage. Imagine that all the keys to success are locked in a safe-deposit box—all but one, that is. One key unlocks the box so that you can get your hands on all the others. That one key is courage, and without courage none of the other keys mean a thing.

The misguided, the deceived, and the fanatical may at times act bravely, hurling themselves into the jaws of death. But true courage, the spontaneous act of self-sacrificial concern for the defenseless, is not fanaticism but character.

The way a society understands courage will, in a great part, determine whether it will be a noble civilization or sink into brutality and chaos. Courage is *not* the feeling of fearlessness. It is rather that willingness of mind necessary to act out of conviction rather than feeling. One may actually feel quite fearless and act in a cowardly manner. Also, one may feel quite fearful and behave with great courage.

However, when we can no longer even identify which situations demand truly courageous responses, then we no longer know when to take a stand. Finally we will lose our understanding of what courage is. If a society misdefines courage, it is on the verge of chaos.

THE COST OF COURAGE

Courage is that willingness to deny my own flesh and do what is right and noble, regardless of the cost. That is why courage is the first and greatest element of character. Merely knowing what is loyal, honest, or true is not enough. It takes courage to *act* on virtue. Courage summons every other virtue into action in the face of temptation or crisis.

For example, a contractor agrees to build a house for a certain amount of money. The contract calls for using top-grade materials. However, a sudden unexpected rise in the cost of materials catches him and many other contractors by surprise. Now, if he fulfills the contract as signed, he knows he will lose money. He also knows he could use a lower grade of material and get away with it. It probably would not even make much difference in the quality of the house. The obvious issue is honesty. He knows the honest thing to do, but his honesty will cost him money. It will require tremendous courage for him to act honestly. Honesty is the virtue that is present, but it will take courage to put it into action.

MORE THAN VALOR

Many miss the greater truth of courage by thinking of it solely in terms of bravery. Though bravery may be admirable, courage is far more than valor in the face of danger. Courage and heroism are not exactly the same. Acts of heroism may or may not be proof of true courage.

Heroism in the face of danger may be a temporary burst of instinct not reflective of true character. Some people are bolder than others by nature. Sometimes public heroes in war or athletics later live unproductive and even destructive lives. Such people were never truly courageous. They were simply brave.

Furthermore, courage without character can descend into mere bravado. The difference between a hero and an obnoxious show-off is character. In other words, if their motives are selfish and impure, a "hero's" actions may result from a lust for fame that overrides good judgment.

Beyond circumstance, past mere bravery, there is another kind of courage. The courage of true character uplifts a life. A warrior may fight valiantly, overcome overwhelming odds, brave all manner of danger, and defeat a superior enemy, only to plunder the city and murder its citizenry. Is he courageous? In every classical and biblical sense of virtue, the answer is a definite no. The fearless warrior who rapes and burns is not

> MANY MISS THE GREATER TRUTH OF COURAGE BY THINKING OF IT SOLELY IN TERMS OF BRAVERY.

courageous. He is a brute. Courage, true courage, is about valiant goodness.

DAILY COURAGE

The long, lingering moral crises of life are the most difficult. Those who stand up day after day under withering criticism need a far greater kind of courage than the once-in-a-lifetime hero. Courage in an enduring crisis is character's most painful and most profound engraver.

> COURAGE IS THAT WILLINGNESS TO DENY MY OWN FLESH AND DO WHAT IS RIGHT AND NOBLE, REGARDLESS OF THE COST.

We all cheer for the professional athlete who plays the Super Bowl in great pain! His is, in a sense, a courageous act. However, he may also be driven by motives such as ego and his next contract.

Consider instead the crippled teenager who wakes up every morning in excruciating pain. She cannot even go to the bathroom alone. Yet every day she thanks God that she has a job to go to. Day in and day out, she does what she can do with fingers that rebel and a body that screams in agony. She may never be thought beautiful, never be pursued by men, never know the tender embrace of a loving husband, and never bear children. Yet day after day after day, despite her pain, she simply does what is right. She is truly courageous. May God give us more like her.

COURAGE AND LEADERSHIP: THREE KINGS IN CRISIS

David, Herod, and Jesus, all leaders and all kings, are a study in contrasts. Three more different kings can hardly be imagined.

Herod was the ultimate tyrant. He was a collaborator as well as a murderous pervert, but the defining crack in his character was cowardice.

David was not just a warrior king. He was *the* warrior king. Larger than history, he lived his life in capital letters. David's victories were monumental, and his failures were just as monumental. Yet at many points in his life he showed tremendous courage under extreme pressure.

Jesus, the gentle shepherd, is probably not seen by many as being particularly courageous. He fought no battles, led no troops, and scaled no fortress walls, yet in His death by execution, we see courage of the highest order.

Scripture gives us a window into the lives of these three kings. By comparing their character under pressure, which is where character is always revealed, we can learn much about courageous and cowardly leadership.

KING HEROD

King Herod, who had stolen his own brother's wife and was living with her openly, was rebuked by John the Baptist. Herod himself lacked the courage to have the prophet beheaded. He ultimately commanded it because of lust, pride, and the fear of looking weak in the eyes of his court. When Herod would have executed John, he lacked even the brutal fearlessness to commit murder. It was not because he feared God, but because he feared the people. Fear robbed him of leadership, as we see in Matthew 14:5–10. Fearful of a treacherous woman, a cowardly king killed a courageous prophet. National character is never as fragile as when leaders are more afraid of men than they are of God. When fearful, lustful fools lead any nation, its character grows weak indeed.

KING DAVID

In 1 Samuel 30:1–6, David's leadership was tested when the city of Ziklag was burned and all the families of his men were taken into slavery. Even David's own family was captured. Leadership is a great challenge. The courageous will not shrink from leadership, but when everything goes badly, courage is tested. When "Ziklag" is burned, when their wives and children are carried away captive, the people long to rise up and blame God, with whom they are angry. Instead, they will often blame their leader. In the painful loneliness of leadership, unless a man has already developed the ability to encourage himself in the Lord, his character will fail the test.

David learned to encourage himself in God as a teenager. When a bear came out of the woods to kill his father's sheep, David said, "In the name of the Lord my God, you won't get these sheep!" He learned to encourage himself in God when all the other shepherds ran off and left the lambs to the lion. David alone rose up from his sleeping mat and wrestled the lion to the ground and killed it. (See 1 Samuel 17:34–35.)

David said, "God is our refuge and strength" (Ps. 46:1.) The Book of Psalms was not written by a man who never knew fear but by a man who, at times, knew deep and terrifying fear. Yet he learned in the face of fear to find ultimate courage in his fear of God. He encouraged himself in the Lord his God.

Standing in the smoldering ruins of Ziklag, the men turned their faces toward David with accusation and anger in their eyes. In that moment, the future of Israel hung by the thread of the courage of a shepherd king. When there is no apparent reason for courage, and God is all that the leader has left, then all he has is everything he needs.

KING JESUS

On the night that He was betrayed, with His friends asleep in the grass, Jesus fell across a stone in a lonely garden and thought of the approaching horror of the cross. Not only the physical agony of crucifixion but also the spiritual nightmare of God-forsakenness loomed before Him. Some may say He felt no fear. The Bible says sweat drops like blood splattered on the stone. Fear wrenched in His guts like a knife. Satanic voices screamed in the night. Finally He cried out to God, "O God, I don't want to do this!" It was only when His soul ached for escape and the air was thick with fear that He uttered his great courageous prayer: "Nevertheless, not my will, but yours, be done" (Luke 22:42).

Jesus denied the screaming demand of His own will, silenced the tortured cry of His own flesh, and rejected fear. He acted in magnificent courage, not awakening His friends, not arming them with swords, and not charging across the Kidron Valley to take Jerusalem by storm. A cavalry charge might seem manly and brave, but in that moment, for Him, for us, it would not have been courageous.

His enemies came for Him with their torches bright against the night sky and their swords rattling at their sides, and the courageous Savior said, "I told you that I am he. So, if you seek me, let these men go" (John 18:8).

"I don't want to do this."

"I know."

"Please let me stay home with you. Please, Mother, I'll be good."

She could see that his eyes were brimming with tears. Ten is such a young age, not one at which a boy should have to deal with things like this. His lip trembled, and he clutched at her sleeve.

"It's not a matter of being good, Sean. You're always good. It's about your life. How long can you stay with me? Don't you know that I want you to? I'd love to keep you right beside me all day, every day. That would make me happy, but it would also make me selfish. No, Sean, you have to go back—back to school, back to life."

"I'm afraid." He was so small, so frail, and so defenseless against a stupid, cruel world full of stupid, cruel children.

"I know."

"Is it all right? To be afraid, I mean."

"Yes. It's all right."

"I don't want to do this."

"That's all right too. It's not in the wanting to or in the feeling brave. It's in the doing it anyway."

"Do you *think they'll laugh at me?"*

She hesitated, wondering how much he could take from her. "Some will, Sean. Some will stare, others will ask idiotic questions, and some will try to help and be friendly and won't know how."

A sob, a sigh, really, deep and full of pain, racked his thin frame. She longed to reach out and hug him, to protect him from this terrible thing, to drive away and keep driving. She clutched the steering wheel and fought to keep from screaming.

"Do you want me to help you get out?"

"No, they're watching."

"I'm proud of you."

He didn't answer but fumbled instead for the door handle. The car at the curb honked, and she struggled to suppress her rage. What did they want her to do, push him out on his face?

The car door swung open, and Sean hoisted himself out, bracing for a moment on the metal crutches and then hefting his weight up onto the curb. With the left crutch he slammed the door and turned to face the knot of children on the school's front steps. For a moment they stared at each other across the uncrossable gulf of different experience—her little son remembering what it was like to have legs, and other people's sons and daughters wondering what it is like not to.

At last, he started toward them, away from her, from the safety of her, swinging his prosthetic legs in rhythm with his crutches.

"I love you," she whispered, knowing he could not hear. "I'm proud of you."

Then the driver behind her honked again, and she shouted at the rearview mirror, "All right, all right. I'm moving, I'm moving."

III

Loyalty—Success in Relationships

An ounce of loyalty is worth a
pound of cleverness.

—Elbert Hubbard

Only once in American history did the head of state of a foreign government surrender his position and the sovereignty of his own nation to unite with the United States. That nation was the Republic of Texas, and its president was Sam Houston.

Adventurer, frontiersman, general, and politician, Sam Houston's name was a household word in Texas and in the United States when Abraham Lincoln was an unknown backwoods lawyer. It is fascinating to note that the Texas Declaration of Independence was signed on Houston's birthday, March 2, 1836. Houston and his army of ragtag volunteers defeated the might of a massive Mexican army. Then, like George

Washington, Houston became the revered first president of the wild and sprawling new nation of Texas.

Less than thirty years later, Texas, now a state, debated whether to join the Confederacy in secession or to remain with the Union it had voluntarily entered in 1845. The vast majority raucously demanded secession. One voice, Houston's, cried out for national loyalty.

The elder statesman of Texas stumped the state to the point of exhaustion. His message was always the same: "The destruction of the Union would be the destruction of all the states."

Shunned by the young hotheads eager for war and dismissed by a new generation who thought him a relic, Houston's pleas for national loyalty were ignored. If Texas had listened, tragedy might have been averted. The refusal of Texas to join the Confederacy might well have dissuaded other states, and the bloodiest nightmare in American history might have been avoided. Unfortunately, Houston's cry to remain in the Union was rejected. Houston, now fatigued and discouraged, must have sensed he was failing physically as well as politically.

"I wish, if this Union must be dissolved, that its ruins may be the monument of my grave, and the graves of my family. I wish no epitaph to be written to tell that I survived the ruin of this glorious Union."

Pressure mounted on the old warrior to take the oath of allegiance to the Confederacy, but Houston's loyalty held. He refused, knowing that it meant the certain end of his political career in the South and isolation for his family. For Houston, loyalty to his nation was stronger than any hope of a political future. He steadfastly refused the oath.

"In the name of the constitution of Texas, which has been trampled upon, I refuse to take this oath. I love Texas too well to bring civil strife and bloodshed upon her."

He saw the beginning of the bloodshed he prophesied, but he did not survive to see its conclusion. Houston was hurt by the rejection of his leadership, deeply saddened by the horrible Civil War, but unaltered in his devotion to his nation. Sam Houston was a

Texan, *the* Texan, but he was, above all things,
a loyal American.[1]

Imagine a business where there is no loyalty. How
could it hope to succeed? Employees who lie about
their travel expenses. Presidents who lie to their
board. Board members who lie to their stockholders. They are all hoping to find quick success. Instead, what they will find is sure failure.

> LOYALTY IS THE GLUE THAT HOLDS RELATIONSHIPS TOGETHER AND MAKES FAMILIES FUNCTIONAL AND ARMIES VICTORIOUS. LOYALTY IS THE FABRIC OF SOCIETY.

Loyalty is the very fabric of community. Without a basic trust in some kind of commitment, relationships cannot prosper. Without loyalty, family, community, and culture will disintegrate.

When loyalty is lost, the very fabric of relationship unravels. No one can translate into relationships a virtue that is fundamentally misunderstood. No society can expect loyalty to anchor its relationships once treachery becomes admirable. The seams of community are ripped apart when treachery becomes an acquired virtue. In a society thus brutalized, no one is safe. Family ties mean little, and friendship means even less. Life without loyalty is fragile in the jungle of betrayal.

Loyalty is not a matter of trading off. One does not gain six points for being loyal to their spouse, then lose three for company disloyalty, finishing at a good solid plus-three. Efforts to isolate certain aspects of life are foolish and dangerous. A man does not simply act disloyally in some particular arena of his life unrelated to the rest. A man is either loyal or he is not.

Loyalty is the willingness, because of relational commitment, to deflect praise, admiration, and success onto another. This loyalty may well be at great personal expense, but it will encourage and bless its object.

Loyalty never steals authority. It refuses to accept inappropriate love or praise that might properly exalt another. Loyalty is the glue that holds relationships together and makes families functional and armies victorious. Loyalty is the fabric of society.

Loyalty is the basic element that cements relationships. If husbands are disloyal to their wives, if children are disloyal to their parents, parents to children, employees to employers, then there is no secure relationship, and the fabric of community soon unravels.

STOLEN HEARTS

Every month, on a certain day, the king's court in Israel was held for people who had exhausted all possibilities of appeals in civil and criminal matters. On that day anyone could appeal directly to King David. His decisions, just or otherwise, were final. Of course, the backlog of appeals soon became tremendous.

David's son Absalom exploited this frustration for his own advantage. Standing tall in his chariot, the strikingly handsome Absalom created quite a stir. As the magnificent chariot rumbled through Jerusalem, Absalom's youthful good looks and flowing hair were admired by men and desired by women. It became his habit to wait at one of the city gates for those coming on the day of the king's court. Flattered at being summoned into Absalom's chariot, the upset people shared openly. He wooed them like a true politician, kissing their babies and consoling their hurts, yet offering no hope that David would prove helpful.

"It's not altogether David's fault," Absalom would explain sarcastically. "He's overworked, to be sure. We all understand that. The problem is that he stubbornly refuses to appoint a deputy. Now if *I* were deputy, or even king, I'd make sure you got justice. The appeal ought to go your way, but with David on the throne, well, who knows?"

The people would bow down before Absalom, and soon they longed for him to be their champion. Absalom's personal embrace in traditional Middle Eastern style was a very symbolic act. Absalom's embrace was calculated to seal their loyalty to him personally. Of course, he had no right to such dedication. Only David had a right to that. "So Absalom stole the hearts of the men of Israel" (2 Sam. 15:6).

The throne was Absalom's by birth. It should have and would have gone to him. His untimely and tragic death, which cost him his destiny, was the unavoidable end of his disloyalty and rebellion. His disloyalty caused his rebellion, and his rebellion cost him his life. When outward rebellion occurs, it is always because loyalty was not added to faith.

Loyalty refuses to accept inappropriate credit, receive improper admiration, or steal the respect due others. Such loyalty is usually carved into a character at no small cost.

THE STRATA OF LOYALTY

A particularly ironic confusion arises from our society's general disregard for the virtue of loyalty. We have become unable to prioritize our loyalties. That is to say, confusion in society results from failure to establish appropriate levels of loyalty. Not all loyalties are created equal. Spheres of loyalty will often conflict. Weakness and instability in character will be the result of failure to distinguish levels of loyalty and resolve this inner conflict. The apostle James wrote, "He is a double-minded man, unstable in all his ways" (James 1:8).

Only by working downward from the ultimate loyalty can this be avoided. By first establishing the nonnegotiable, which can never be denied, the tension is eased at descending levels. Once that loyalty among all loyalties is settled, questions of conflict are more easily resolved.

A woman with whom I once counseled was awaiting her criminal trial for embezzlement. She had gotten involved with a man who was heavily in debt. He had pleaded with her to get some money for him or he would go to prison. She embezzled a substantial amount of money from her job to help him, fully intending to repay it. The scandal of her arrest was a bitter shock to her church and her family. When I asked how she could have fallen for such a tired old line, she responded that she had no idea.

She was right! She had no idea. By allowing a secondary loyalty to her boyfriend to replace her ultimate loyalty to Jesus Christ, she had entered into sin and serious criminal activity. She excused her disloyalty to her God and to her employer by hiding behind loyalty to a man, and not much of a man at that.

The Disloyalty of Criticism

In criticizing the wisdom and ability of a superior, a subordinate lowers himself. Logic dictates that the lesser works for the greater. Therefore if the boss is the champion nitwit of all time, what kind of people would work for him? If the boss is an all-around great person of tremendous insight and wisdom, the happy conclusion is that surely he likely showed wisdom in his hiring decisions. When I lift up my boss, I am lifted up. When I brag on my wife, I shall be held in honor by others. If I speak of her disloyally, others will agree with me that she certainly is stupid—stupid enough to marry me! Likewise, if my parents are the village idiots, well, they raised me.

> There are few virtues in the kingdom more honored by God than loyalty.

The Supernatural Power of Loyalty

The redemptive grace of loyalty is so powerful it can literally fill any situation with healing and miraculous blessings. Any force that powerful, however, cannot be violated without dire consequences. There are few virtues in the kingdom more honored by God than loyalty. Absalom's doom was sealed by his disloyalty to David, but David's loyalty to an unworthy Saul confirmed his destiny for the throne.

In the household of Naaman, a Syrian general, there lived a young Jewish slave girl. She had been captured by a Syrian raiding party. Stolen from her family, alone in a foreign land, she served as a personal slave to Naaman's wife, hardly a circumstance to inspire loyalty. Even the most outwardly obedient slave might murder his master mentally. Yet this little girl chose to be loyal with her whole heart. Somehow her family in Israel had carved loyalty into her character at a tender age. Now a slave in Syria, her well-shaped character found genuine concern for the one who owned her just as he owned his horse.

When Naaman contracted leprosy, the slave girl told her mistress, "Would that my lord were with the prophet [Elisha] who is in Samaria! He would cure him of his leprosy" (2 Kings 5:3).

Amazing! She sent him who held her captive to her home country, where she surely wanted to be. She sent him to be set free of his disease, though he held her in slavery. She genuinely wanted Naaman to be healed, and he was. The miracle that Naaman received by the ministry of Elisha never would have happened without that slave girl's unlikely loyalty.

Grateful for the miraculous healing, Naaman offered Elisha a large reward, which Elisha declined. Elisha's servant and understudy Gehazi shook his head in amazement. The Syrian had been miraculously healed! "Why shouldn't Elisha be blessed?" Gehazi reasoned in his heart.

Elisha refused the luxurious gifts of the Syrian, but Gehazi would not. He waited until Naaman was out of Elisha's sight, and then he raced after the foreign general. Elisha had changed his mind, Gehazi explained to the Syrian. Two visiting prophets had arrived, and Elisha would now be happy to accept some gifts after all. Naaman was only too delighted to give.

Elisha, however, discerned the deception and struck the hapless Gehazi with leprosy. In other words, if Gehazi wanted the Syrian's money, then by all means he should have the Syrian's disease as well.

The greed of Gehazi is obvious. The issue of disloyalty is more easily overlooked. For personal gain he misrepresented his employer's motives. Acting out of self-interest, he denied his superior's nobility, goals, purpose, and will. What an ironic contrast!

A slave girl's character and loyalty brought miraculous healing and blessing, while the disloyalty of a prophet in training brought scandal, disease, and death. Loyalty is a gemstone virtue whose luster, in a golden setting of faithfulness, brings glory to God and health to all it touches.

Tears rolled down Tiffany's dimpled cheeks and fell in dark droplets on her Dior blouse. She wiped halfheartedly at them with the back of her hand. Devastated. She was absolutely devastated. Marcie was her friend, her very best friend in all the world, or at least she was supposed to be. But there it was, in black and white, so to speak. It was hideous. She had told Marcie and only Marcie. No one would have ever known if Marcie had just kept her promise to keep it secret. Secret? What a joke. Instead, Marcie put the story on her MySpace page for the whole world to read.

"Do you see it?"

Tiffany had almost forgotten that Amber was still on the phone, and her voice so startled her that she nearly dropped her new iPhone she had gotten for her birthday.

"Of course, I can see it, Amber. I'm looking right at it. I can't believe it. I've never felt so betrayed in my whole life."

"I know how you feel, Tiff." Amber's voice was encouraging. "A loyal friend is really hard to find."

"Yeah," Tiffany sobbed. "Loyalty of any kind. Does it even exist anymore? I think I hate disloyalty more than anything. It's like murder or something. Anyway, that's how I feel."

"Tiffany, you have to tell your mom."

"She'll never understand. I'll be grounded till I'm thirty."

"No, you won't. Your mom is cool. Everybody says so."

"No," Tiffany sobbed. "No, she's not. She's a cruel, old witch, and she doesn't even try to understand me."

"Tiffany," Amber said as a note of seriousness came into her voice, "you shouldn't talk about your mother like that. You know she's…"

"No, she isn't," Tiffany wailed. "She's not what you think. She doesn't care about me. She never buys me anything or supports me. She only thinks about herself, and I hate her. No, I do. I hate her."

IV

DILIGENCE—SUCCESS IN WORK

Diligence in employments of less consequence is the most successful introduction to greater enterprises.

—SIR FRANCIS DRAKE

The sickly, squalling slave baby was handed over to one of the elderly women. No one—not the plantation owner, Mr. Moses Carver, nor the slave woman in whose arms he screamed—no one saw any hope for the child. What hope could there be for George Washington Carver, an African American baby born in the waning days of the Civil War and orphaned when his father died and his mother was kidnapped by slave stealers?

The frail lad's earliest years were spent in poor physical health, but he was mentally and spiritually strong. There was no school for African Americans in Diamond Grove, Missouri, but the young boy learned to read on his own. Hours spent, on his own initiative, mastering spelling and grammar reaped a great reward. By age ten, George Carver was moving from town to town, seeking out anyone who would feed his ravenous appetite for knowledge.

When, at the age of sixteen, George Carver became the first African American admitted to Iowa A&M (now Iowa State University), his early education was the fruit of diligent self-application. Excellent marks, a charming personality, and a commitment to servant-leadership made him an academic and social success at college. After graduate school he became the first African American admitted to Iowa A&M's faculty.

Carver subsequently left Iowa to join Booker T. Washington at Tuskegee Institute, where he found international fame for his work in agricultural research. It was not his scholarship alone, however, that endeared him to his students, his colleagues, and the world. Carver's unflagging commitment to excellence, to diligently see the job finished and finished right was the foundation upon which he built a life of worth.

> Born a slave and an orphan, George
> Washington Carver proved that character can
> lift a life above its beginnings. He was a man
> of diligence who could not be defeated by a
> whole world of obstacles.[1]

We are often tempted to think of success in terms of some great triumph. We think that one "big deal" will make us famous and successful: "After my appearance on *American Idol*, I will be discovered. Someone will see my talent and lift me up from obscurity to success." However, true success is most often for most of us not a "big deal" at all; instead, it is a lifetime of "little deals," like paying attention to detail and doing the small jobs right over and over and over again.

This is a perverse society indeed that celebrates the occasional genius and scorns the diligent. How strange that we so honor the gifted, who are what they are without effort or sacrifice. What honor is due them?

Modern America has placed a premium on talent while virtues like diligence are ignored. In so doing we promote characterlessness. The modern American sees work as the curse of the masses. The faithful, diligent journeyman is mocked as an unimaginative moron unworthy to be in the same room with the royalty of creative genius, even if that genius is corrupt, unproductive, and undisciplined. Those who are hardworking and disciplined often go unrewarded while temperamental and characterless "geniuses" are elevated.

American industry is rapidly gaining a reputation for creative ideas that will not work and a lazy, undisciplined workforce that cannot produce. American industry is confused by its own traditions. We have been taught that, despite slipshod methods, disregard for diligence, and short-run, quick-fix tactics, American creativity will somehow make it all come together at the last minute.

> DILIGENCE LEADS
> TO BALANCED,
> SUCCESSFUL LIVING.

We stare disillusioned at vehicles that will not run, savings and loans that fail, ministries that do not last, and companies that go bankrupt. In the

1950s, American industry laughed at pitiful Japanese efforts to mimic us. With classical Oriental diligence they set to work. Creative research and development, they said, will come. Later we will innovate, but first, they maintained, we must work. They proved to be true what we once knew. Genius is a fragile substitute for character.

Likewise, American education has squandered its soul and its power. We are now reaping the bitter harvest of a generation of useless theory. Our schools and universities continue to spew out graduates who can explain the Peyote cult and do African folk dances but cannot hold down jobs. The university campus, we are told, is to be the marketplace of ideas. What about the idea that diligence is not the last resort of the boring and unimaginative? Diligence is the virtue that leads to balanced, successful living. Theory is no substitute for practice, and creativity without character will quickly corrupt.

When a class is studying Edgar Allan Poe's brooding prose, why not teach the young to learn from his destruction and get a heart of wisdom? In addition to studying Poe's works, we must mourn the unwritten stories washed away by booze. Instead of producing young musicians who have merely mastered Mozart's concertos, can we no longer marry character to genius so as to defeat Mozart's demons? The genius of Mozart must be recognized. His pathetic waste is a cautionary tale to the wise. While studying the art of Van Gogh, we must dare to speculate on masterpieces never painted because of debauchery. Diligence is the virtue that sets us free to fulfill our creative destiny.

DILIGENCE AS STEADY APPLICATION

Steady application may not necessarily raise the peaks of the super performer, but it can put a foundation under him to reduce the depth of his valleys. Furthermore, it enables "Steady Freddy" to reach his potential. The diligent man is a steady performer, and the steady performer is a *finisher*.

Well-meaning zealots may say, "I am called to missions. I know I'm supposed to give two weeks' notice, I also owe some money, and my dad cosigned on my car, but God is telling me to go into the mission field—right now!" No, He is not! God is calling all of us to be diligent, faithful finishers. If we cannot be trusted to pay our debts, how can He trust us to save Africa?

For good or ill, we always impact with our own character those things committed to us. As we are engraved with the image of Christ, all those areas in which we have stewardship must also bear the stamp of His character.

DILIGENCE AS IMMEDIATE OBEDIENCE

Diligence not only finishes the job, but it also does so without unnecessary delay. Paul called it being "ready" (2 Tim. 4:2).

It is a true character-shaping virtue to do it now. Procrastination is not merely a personality weakness. Procrastination is a sin and a sign of spiritual backsliding. The diligent have disciplined themselves to hear from authority and obey now. Hence, when God speaks, the diligent are the very ones who hear and obey now. Children must be taught that if they cannot obey parents whom they can see, they will never learn to obey God, whom they cannot see.

There is another and even more menacing danger in procrastination. As we procrastinate, we begin to believe that God also is a procrastinator. The Word of God teaches that God, who is faithful, will execute judgment in His own time. When it happens, it will come suddenly. We dare not project our slackness on God. A generation with no fear of authority becomes less diligent. Laziness and sloth breed sin and rebellion, but authority lacks the willpower to be diligent in punishment. To such a people, the wrath of God seems unrealistic, if not laughable, and, at the very least, avoidable.

DILIGENCE AS EXACTITUDE

Ezra 7:23 says, "Whatever is decreed by the God of heaven, let it be done in full ["exactly," ASV] for the house of the God of heaven, lest his wrath be against the realm of the king and his sons."

In other words, do it now, do it exactly as instructed, and do it until it is finished. America's romance with creative individualism has often worked to a disadvantage in this regard. The free-thinking lone wolf is often celebrated while the obedient and diligent are mocked.

One concept that the immature have difficulty grasping is that doing a secular job well, exactly as instructed, has an enduring spiritual impact on character. There is a connection between the way I do my job or clean my room and my relationship with God. If I do the things required of me in an angry and rebellious manner, diligence is not being carved into my character. The task may get completed, but my character remains unchanged. When anybody believes that diligence in worldly matters is of no spiritual value, his own spirit suffers.

Negative spiritual lessons are learned when obedience and diligence are held to be unimportant. When God calls on the man without diligence, he will prove unfit. He may delay. He may do it halfway. He may improvise. Eventually, however, he will fail the test. Partial obedience is disobedience. Delayed obedience is disobedience.

Character does it promptly. Character does it exactly as told. Character finishes it.

Diligence as Carefulness

To be diligent also means to use care. For example, the young stock clerk is told, "Stack these five boxes." He may do it quickly and complete the task, yet fail utterly by breaking everything in the boxes. In this sense, diligence has to do with attitude as well as action. We must do every job as unto the Lord. I must make my job as important to me as it is to my employer, or I sin against him or her.

Throughout the time I was in college, my wife and I worked hard to make ends meet. I often worked at two or three jobs doing whatever I could do to raise the next semester's tuition. At one job in a grocery store, I worked alongside two other guys. One was a hotshot local basketball star. His coach had arranged for him to get the job there in order to pick up some spending money. He thought it was a lark, so he played at the job. The other fellow, Tom, had a slight mental disability. The basketball player constantly made Tom the butt of every joke. Yet I learned much by watching that boy with a mental disability bag groceries. Whether there was one person or fifty persons in line, he never altered his course. He would carefully place one can at a time in the sack, not allowing pressure to force him into error. He never hurried. He never got flustered. He never tried to move faster than he could do the job efficiently.

The basketball player was six-foot-nine and marvelously coordinated. When he wanted to, he could bag groceries like a whirlwind. With one hand he could bag groceries faster than Tom could with both hands at top speed. Then the athlete would start clowning or be in the back taking a break when he was supposed to be bagging groceries. Worse still, he was rude to the boss and to customers. I have seldom been as delighted as I was to watch as the manager fired that basketball star. He fired him right in front of us all, including Tom. I will never forget that manager pointing his finger at the boy with a mental disability and saying to that basketball star, "You see this kid? You don't think much of him, do you? He is worth his weight in gold, and you're not worth a dime."

I learned a character lesson in that grocery store. Just be the best you can be. Just put the groceries in the bag one can at a time. Just finish. Just do it right. Just do it with care. Tom cared about the job. He wanted to do it right. He felt a responsibility to the grocery store. He handled a can of tomatoes as if it were a live baby. The basketball player dropped crates and burst open boxes. He deserved to be fired.

Diligence is also important in relationships. We must be sensitive to others, aware of what is going on around us. The diligent who learn to be observant of others seldom have to apologize later for being thoughtless.

Diligence and Temptation

The diligent will also be stronger in the face of those surprise temptations that arise suddenly to defeat so many. Everyone will be caught unaware from time to time, but those who are diligent in the things of the world tend toward diligence in the things of the Spirit. The lion is not nearly so able to leap out from hiding and destroy the diligent with unexpected temptations.

> DILIGENCE IS THE RESPONSIBLE, ORDERLY, STEADY APPLICATION OF GOD'S POWER WITHIN ME TOWARD WHATEVER RESPONSIBILITY IS MINE.

Recently I counseled a young man whose girlfriend was pregnant. He said, "We never intended this to happen."

Of course, they never intended it! That, however, was the very cause of the problem. The young couple was not intentional. They did not intend to sin; they were swept into it by passion. The lack of intentionality caused them to be caught in a situation where they failed morally. Through lack of diligence, sin became unavoidable. Sexuality is a tremendous force. Our teens must learn to show respect for its power. Look ahead at the situation. Be observant to possible danger and avoid it.

I have been all around the world and seen all kinds of things. I have never heard of anybody getting pregnant in a prayer meeting. We often drift into sin because of simply not being observant. We must remain alert to the danger in any situation.

THE FOUR FACES OF DILIGENCE

The virtue of diligence has four faces:

1. Diligence means *constancy*. Temporary obedience is disobedience.

2. Diligence is *instant*. Delayed obedience is disobedience.

3. Diligence is *exactitude*. Partial obedience is disobedience.

4. Diligence is *observant care*. Careless obedience is disobedience.

Diligence is the responsible, orderly, steady application of God's power within me toward whatever responsibility is mine.

Mountain High School's battered old Blue Bird bus was symbolic of the track team it carried. The ancient vehicle seemed to be held together with wire. It was not pretty, and it looked like a relic from another era, but it ran fairly well and got where it was supposed to go.

Bouncing along on the torn green seats inside, the little team attempted in vain to act confident and relaxed. On the front seat, gruff old Coach Hardeman pretended to be dozing. His hat was shoved forward over his eyes, and his arms were folded across his chest. Mr. Wheelwright, the good-natured school janitor who doubled as the bus driver and campus grandpa, whistled the same nondescript tune he had been whistling for years.

The boys were mostly quiet except for the occasional outburst when a spit-wad found its mark or when some halfhearted insult earned reaction. They were intimidated. In fact, they were terrified. Never in Mountain High's inglorious athletic history had any of its teams made it to the state meet. Many of the boys had never seen Lexington. Blue Rock, Kentucky, seemed insignificant to them as they stared out at the huge city. It made them feel insignificant as well. Despite the forced cheerfulness, several wished they had not come.

57

Suddenly Coach Hardeman sat up straight, pushed back his hat, and stretched his arms above his head. Spinning to face the boys, he stared down the length of the shabby old bus. He searched the face of each of his skinny charges.

"This here's a big city, ain't it?" he asked.

The boys muttered their agreement, staring vacantly out the windows.

"I don't reckon we gonna win every event," he continued. "But no school in the state is gonna win 'em all. The main thing is, you're here! This is an invitational, and you were all invited. You deserve to be here."

"We'll do our best, coach," Donny shouted.

"Yeah, I know you will." The coach smiled as he spoke.

"Coach, what about the long-distance race?" Harold asked. "Craig's home with the mumps." This last comment, which was a fact everyone knew, brought forth a burst of laughter.

"I'm glad you asked that, Harold, because I have a surprise for everyone. Beau is going to run it."

All eyes turned to the face of the senior water boy. Year after year Beau went out for the track team, only to be made the manager. Beau grinned sheepishly from *the back seat and shrugged his shoulders.*

"But coach..." Cass objected.

"No buts! All of you have your own events. I asked him, and he agreed. That's that." The coach set his lips in a firm line.

From the back, somebody muttered, "He can't win. Heck, he can't even place high."

"I didn't ask him to win or place high. I only asked him to finish," the coach answered as Beau, water boy, turned to gaze without expression at the passing traffic.

The day went pretty much as expected. Mountain High placed third in the 100-yard dash and fourth in the 440 relay. That was it. As they began repacking their gear, they heard the top-ten finishers in the long distance race being announced as they crossed the line.

Out of a statewide field of one hundred runners, finishing tenth was an accomplishment. But Beau's name was not among the ten.

The lights began to dim as the last of the spectators drifted toward the parking lot. The Mountain High boys stared in confusion at Coach Hardeman. He was gesturing madly at the head official. The two men's voices were loud, nearly shouting, but the boys could not hear the words. The rugged mob of Appalachian teens drifted closer to the argument.

"All right!" they heard the official shout. "We'll turn the lights back on. But it makes no sense. The track meet's over. Just call him in."

"No," Hardeman said. "I told him to finish. Let him finish."

"All right, all right," the official muttered. "Turn 'em on," he shouted up to the control tower by the press box. "Turn the lights back on!"

Only when the stadium lights came back to full power did they see him. Struggling around the far turn was Beau. His arms dangled limply at his sides. His frail legs barely moved. The boy's head wobbled pitiably.

They stared at him in disbelief. The return of lights drew the attention of the few remaining spectators loitering at the gates, and they began drifting back toward the infield. The lone figure laboring up the cinder track moved toward the finish line in obvious agony. Gasping for breath, the boy struggled with each step.

As the cluster of spectators grew, the Mountain High track team became aware of the comments of the adults around them.

"Look at that."

"Why doesn't he quit?"

"I never saw anything like it."

Suddenly somebody cheered. More cheers. Oblivious to the rising cheers, Beau Rogers tried to concentrate on nothing but the finish line. His legs were screaming in pain. He knew he was close to vomiting. Still he came. Right. Left. Right. Left.

He collapsed across the finish line and into his coach's arms. The team swarmed around him, shouting and jumping on him as if he had just won an Olympic gold medal. As the boy lay back against Coach Hardeman's arm, he became aware of the excitement around him.

"What are they cheering about, coach?" he whispered.

"They're cheering for you, son. They're cheering you."

It made no sense to the boy. What did it mean?

"I finished, coach, just like you said," he answered.

"Yeah, Beau, that's right."

V

MODESTY—SUCCESS AND SIMPLICITY

Nothing can atone for the lack of modesty; without which beauty is ungraceful and wit detestable.

—Sir Richard Steele

How's your boy, Bob?" asks the tall, slim man in the plaid shirt.

"Fine, Mr. Blanchard," answers a burly truck driver with a day's growth of beard. "He took a turn for the good last week."

"Well, we're praying."

There is nothing unusual or spectacular about this brief conversation in the graveled parking lot of a Christian men's retreat in South Georgia. Two men—a businessman and a truck driver—exchange greetings and prayerful concerns with the casual ease of equals and fellow travelers. Nothing exceptional. Nothing at all, until you realize that "Mr. Blanchard" is James H. Blanchard, CEO and chairman of the board of Synovus.

Phenomenally successful in business and extremely influential in politics, Blanchard dislikes any hint of flamboyance and extravagance. Approachable, humble, and a fiercely dedicated Christian, James Blanchard lives where he was born, in Columbus, Georgia. He has resisted calls to move Synovus (a banking credit card empire worth more than $20 billion) to New York. "Columbus is home," he says, in his soft, aristocratic Southern drawl, as if that explains everything.

Now able to take his place among America's most successful businessmen, James Blanchard remains unimpressed with himself. As comfortable on a bass lake as he is in a boardroom, more concerned with the truck driver's son than he is with the stock market, James Blanchard's modesty has endeared him to the locals.

A convenience store owner in Columbus said of the banking magnate, "Blanchard is real people."

That is perhaps the highest compliment for a truly modest man. Blanchard, while quietly comfortable with his own success, walks in cool balance, falling neither to prideful self-promotion nor to the false humility of the inwardly arrogant.

He just is who he is, a successful man, blessed of God, using the resources at his command for God and for good. Resisting the flashy flamboyance of many less wealthy than himself, Blanchard walks in authentic modesty.[1]

It is one thing to find success. It is quite another to handle it. Success has ruined at least as many as failure has. The athlete who thinks he is above the law, the starlet who flaunts her body and her addictions in public, and the arrogant CEO who parades his triumphs on talk shows have all forgotten how to *stay* successful. The key to that is modesty.

LIVING WITHIN LIMITS

Most modern Americans understand the word *modesty* to have reference only to one's manner of dress, and even then it is mostly used with regard to women. Yet modesty actually has far more to do with self-control and self-respect than with how revealing one's garments are. Style of dress is an aspect of modesty, not a definition.

Modesty, in its classical sense, means living within limits. Modesty submits to the boundaries of decency. It is the opposite of being "bold-eyed," putting oneself forward in the sense of being overly aggressive or conceited. Modesty has to do with being other than boastful and arrogant.

> MODESTY, IN ITS CLASSICAL SENSE, MEANS LIVING WITHIN LIMITS.

Modesty springs from a humble estimation of one's own importance. It is unassuming, but it is not bashful. Modesty acknowledges the fact that there are limits of propriety on life and that it is good to submit to those. Modesty sees restraints as being positive safeguards, not negative obstacles.

Immodesty denies responsibility to law, culture, authority, and tradition. Immodesty is personally offended by signs that say "Keep Off the Grass." Modesty says, "There are things in this world that are right for me to do and things in this world that are not right for me to do. I am not too good or too big or too rich or too powerful for someone else to point those out to me."

Modesty is not mindless subjection to oppression. It is rather the conviction that there are correct limits on life. In addition, the modest learn to set their own limits. Modesty has a great deal to do with one's self-view.

There is a great insight on modesty in Romans 12:1–3. Paul says, "I appeal to you therefore, brothers, to present your bodies as a living sacrifice, holy and acceptable to God" (Rom. 12:1). Obviously, then, we are precious. We are important to God. Otherwise the sacrifice of our lives would be totally unacceptable to Him. If your body is a sacrifice that is acceptable to God, then treating your body with respect is also important to God.

Verse 3 says, "Do not think of yourself more highly than you ought" (NIV).

In other words, a sacrifice is acceptable to God only as long as it is on the altar. When it is presented unto God, it finds its meaning. Withdrawn from the altar of God in arrogant, self-ownership, your body loses its meaning and therefore its value.

Therefore, in being yielded as a sacrifice under the ownership and lordship of Jesus Christ, I find meaning and explanation. When I take my body and my life in my own hands, I make myself meaningless and valueless. My life becomes an unending search for ways to convince myself and the world of my significance.

> AN INNER CONVICTION TO SEEK MODESTY REQUIRES CHRISTIANS TO LOOK IN THE MIRROR AND HONESTLY ASK THEMSELVES SOME SEARCHING QUESTIONS.

Modesty is unassuming and genuinely humble. The immodest announce by behavior, dress, and attitude, to everyone in general and to the opposite sex in particular, "Look at me. I am what is important in this place."

MODESTY AND CONTROLLED LIVING

Modesty also keeps its emotions under appropriate control. There is an emotional immodesty that indulges itself in excessive displays of emotion. To the emotionally immodest, their every tragedy is the worst thing that has ever happened to anybody. Where a balanced person may be mildly happy, the immodest are careening off the walls. Emotions need expression, but the acceptance of limits is the key to balance. There are certain limits outside of which the expression of emotions is improper and even dangerous.

Modesty teaches that it is not necessary for a thirteen-year-old boy to enter every room like an entire roller derby team. Boys must be taught that doors need not be kicked open. On the other hand, we dare not squelch their childlike enthusiasm for life. Modesty is not passionless living. It is passion under control; it is passion that accepts the limits of decency.

We usually think of modesty mainly in connection with clothing and fashion. It is uselessly legalistic to ask such questions as how short is too short and how sheer is too sheer. The more important questions about modest dress have to do with being showy or inappropriately seeking attention. In that sense, then, one might have an immodest hairstyle that is excessive and flamboyant and demands attention.

Modesty that is judgmental will become legalistic to say the least. It is false modesty that nitpicks and criticizes youthful enthusiasm and discourages joy and vitality. Such hypocrisy is hateful and binds people up.

GUIDELINES TO MODESTY

Many Christians ask what styles of dress, makeup, and hair are acceptable, but listing is petty, soon dated, and may miss the point entirely. On the other hand, some guidelines to modesty may be helpful.

- Always be suspicious of the flamboyant. Remember you are trying to express the orderly, decent, modest glory of God through the way you dress.

- Instantly suspect fads.

- In clothing, particularly, try to avoid those styles that are provocative and draw attention to your body.

Now again it must be stated that there is a balance. Holiness does not always have to look like it has been thrown away. We have been through that in generations past. The point is that an inner conviction to seek modesty requires Christians to look in the mirror and honestly ask themselves some searching questions: Are these clothes just slightly too tight? Is this dress just a little too low-cut? Will these clothes be an unnecessary temptation to others? Modesty is the quiet, dignified celebration of the sacredness of one's privacy with God.

God is for the body. The body is holy, a living sacrifice, acceptable unto God. Modesty does not want to inspire the unhealthy attention of others. It does not want to be the center of attention. Modesty—true, balanced, and wholesome modesty—wants Jesus to be the center of attention.

It would be easy if the "Ninety-seven Rules From God About Modesty" were to descend from heaven. That is what the Pharisees thought they had. They were wrong and, in their wrongness, became legalistic and hateful. There are no rules like that because God will not give them. Instead, we must make decisions about makeup, clothing, attire, and all related matters because our hearts are His home and our bodies are a living sacrifice to Him.

As she passed the full-length mirror, Kristy checked herself out. She was transfixed by what she saw. She was very pretty, if not actually beautiful. Even better than beautiful, however, Kristy was rich and beautiful.

Her hair was exactly as she wanted it, though she complained about it constantly. Her sweater-shirt was obviously expensive and fashionable. The top two buttons were open, and the braided gold chain that delicately graced her smooth neck lay across her upper chest. From the chain dangled a seven-hundred-dollar cross with a beautiful little diamond. Her father had complained that it was too expensive for a teenager's necklace, but her mother had successfully interceded as usual. After all, a girl's sixteenth birthday comes only once. It wasn't as if her father could not afford it.

Kristy opened the sweater's third button, revealing a shapely figure. The teenager knotted her brow, wrinkled her nose, and pursed her lips in the cute pout with which she consistently charmed most males and many females. She rebuttoned the sweater, pouted again, and finally unbuttoned it yet again and pulled the sides open just a tiny bit more.

The cross looked absolutely tantalizing on her upper chest. There, that was better. Anyway, the cross should show. It was a birthday present. After all, it was a cross, and everybody in town knew her family was very prominent at First Church. She was not ashamed of that. She tossed her head, corrected her posture, and swirled from the mirror, out of the girls' bathroom and into the lonely hall.

A few quick strides later Kristy stood at the door of the yearbook office. The rest of the committee was inside. She knew they had already been working for three quarters of an hour and were likely to be unreasonable with her. She would fix that. With her hand on the doorknob, she carefully arranged her most dazzling smile, absolutely confident of its effect.

She threw open the door and danced in, nonchalantly tossing her purse onto a nearby desk.

"Sorry I'm late," she sang out to the room in general.

"What else is new?" answered Carl "the Nerd."

She flashed him her most wounded look but said nothing, waiting for others to try to make her feel better. They did not. Instead, the six other teenagers continued their work with hardly a notice of her presence.

"Hi, Kristy," said Elizabeth, the yearbook editor. A chorus of half a dozen "hellos" followed, but they were shockingly halfhearted. Kristy seethed at being so blatantly ignored. Were they trying to punish her for being late?

"Well, I see I'm not needed," Kristy muttered petulantly.

"Sure you are," Elizabeth said patiently. "There's enough work for all of us. Why not trim those pictures on that desk?"

"OK," Kristy answered quietly. She really did not like Elizabeth. Elizabeth was pretty in a way, but she just did so little with herself. Elizabeth was what Kristy's father called a "real little lady." The phrase made Kristy sick, but she felt she should be seen with Elizabeth occasionally. The girl was well liked and extremely smart.

Kristy ambled over to the desk littered with pictures, sat down, and listlessly began the required trimming. She had learned over the years that being barefooted in a room full of people with shoes on always got attention. She thought it made her look free and uninhibited. She lifted both feet and let her pumps drop to the tile floor with a very satisfying clatter. At the noise, several boys glanced at Kristy. Now Kristy studiously ignored them.

She propped her feet on a chair and lounged

backward, pretending to be absorbed in the scissor work. She knew she was finally starting to get some attention. Sitting like that with her feet up, more of her legs would be exposed. Well, who cares? She was just being herself. Could she help it if they looked?

Kristy knew her father would not have liked it. If he could see her now, he would fume just as he did whenever she wore shorts to night church services. He was sweet, but he was also completely out of it, she thought. In a few minutes three of the boys were at her desk, and Elizabeth, Carl "the Nerd," and that Vietnamese girl were working alone at the other.

Kristy's father wanted her to be more like Elizabeth. No, thank you! Anyway, Kristy was a Christian girl. Her father ought to be happy. She wasn't smoking weed. She just didn't let musty old rules get in the way of her happiness. After all, "Where the Spirit of the Lord is, there is liberty." That was the motto verse for her youth group, and she liked it.

Kristy glanced at Elizabeth there at the editor's desk. The girl sat quietly, earnestly doing her work. Oh, Elizabeth was just a bore. Worse than that, Kristy knew that for some unknown reason Elizabeth disapproved of her. How could that be? Kristy was one of the nicest girls in the school.

VI

FRUGALITY—SUCCESS AND PROSPERITY

Frugality is founded on the principle that all riches have limits.

—EDMUND BURKE

When Oseola McCarty was in the sixth grade, she dropped out of elementary school to become the principal caregiver for her dying aunt. She never returned to school, working instead doing laundry and ironing for Hattiesburg, Mississippi's aristocracy. In 1920, a twelve-year-old African American with a sixth-grade education had little to look forward to but hard work.

Oseola McCarty turned her life of service into an anthem to character. Caring for her aunt, then her grandmother, and finally her mother, Oseola became the family hospice. She supported herself and her relatives with her work as a cook and domestic, and, in the process, she earned herself a public reputation as trustworthy, loyal, and diligent.

In private, where no one except some local bankers could see, Oseola McCarty was carving into her youthful character a strength that was eventually to benefit many. Year after year, for more than seven decades, she lived and learned true frugality even on her marginal income. Living at what some would call a poverty level, she still saved. In local banks, buying CDs, setting aside small but regular deposits, Oseola McCarty found herself at the age of eighty-eight, prepared and empowered to do grandly what she had done her whole life.

In July 1995, a humble washerwoman who never attended junior high school presented the University of Southern Mississippi with a check for $150,000. An endowed scholarship for minority students now helps others to an education she never received.

A stunned USM administrator said, "This is by far the largest gift ever given to USM by an African American. We are overwhelmed and humbled by what she has done."

A life of character—a humble, hard-working, sacrificial life built on the conviction that servanthood is noble and important—now enables a new generation to find success through education. The character of Oseola McCarty, however, is her most enduring contribution. Out of a lifetime of laundry, sometimes earning only a dollar a bundle, Oseola McCarty, in quiet character, earned, served, and saved that others might receive.[1]

I once heard a man brag, actually brag, that he had made and lost three fortunes. To find some temporary financial "moment in the sun" is not success. Long-term stability, the kind of success that builds an inheritance and leaves a legacy, is another matter all together. Frugality, not flamboyance, is the key to that kind of success.

Frugality is that virtue, the absence of which touches the very substance of life, and poverty of every kind will follow. Indeed, it will be even worse than that. A society without frugality loses its ability to even understand what is really precious.

If the precious, the semi-precious, and the ordinary all look the same to a society, it becomes impossible to tell the difference between humanity and plastic. A society is defined by what it wastes as well as by what it wants.

FRUGAL OR STINGY

It is difficult to teach frugality to young people because often the very word has utterly disappeared from their vocabulary. Among those in whose vocabulary it does remain, there is a great deal of confusion about what it really means.

Many identify frugality as mere thriftiness, but the thrifty can easily become stingy, then loveless, judgmental, and withholding. Stinginess separates us from those who look to us for care. Frugality springs from a balanced view of things and life. Stinginess may actually be a lack of frugality. What passes for frugality is sometimes only an obsession with smallness and pettiness.

I had a friend in college, Dennis, who prided himself on being frugal. Actually, he was dangerously obsessed with money. I remember the great issue of shoelaces in our sophomore year. Before it was over, I was quite sick of Dennis and his shoelaces. He broke a shoelace, and it became a federal case. He complained for two weeks, not so much because the shoelace had broken, since he had worn it for years and thought it was about time for it to break, but because he could only find shoelaces for sale in pairs. This he resented bitterly. How he moaned, "I don't need two. I only need one." He blamed the entire American industrial system for

> A SOCIETY WITHOUT FRUGALITY LOSES ITS ABILITY TO EVEN UNDERSTAND WHAT IS REALLY PRECIOUS.

selling shoelaces only in pairs. That is not frugality, and it is not a virtue. It is an obsession with pettiness, and God hates petty living.

False frugality always sees itself as acting righteously by doing things that are ridiculous and immoral. Penny-wise and dollar-poor can become a way of life that destroys homes, relationships, and businesses.

Stinginess can also become judgmental toward what it sees to be the excesses of others. A frugal lifestyle is a virtue, but the law of love must preside over our attitudes toward the possessions of others. In other words, God may give another liberty at one level regarding possessions that He does not give me. I have neither the right nor the discernment to decide what God is saying to another. Legalistic judgments about others will make me arrogant and snobby. Law separates people. Frugality is not about imposing laws on each other, but rather it is about hearing from God for ourselves. Frugality is character's attempt to cultivate a lifestyle pleasing in His sight and effective in our pursuit of both holiness and prosperity.

True Frugality

To speak of being frugal implies far more than saving money. Frugality is not the opposite of generosity. It is rather the opposite of reckless extravagance. Frugality, like modesty, has to do with controlled living. The great point of frugality concerns the purpose of things. Frugality is not so much a question of how many things I own but of their purpose and place in my life.

There is, for example, a purpose for leisure in life. Recreation is to rebuild, to re-*create*. It has a function in life. Everyone needs times to recuperate from stress and fatigue. We need times when we do something just for the fun of it, just to relax and have a good time. When frugality is lost, however, recreation gets out of balance.

Consumption without frugality produces an escalating cycle of things without purpose. Thus the power of mammon eats into our lifestyle and our character. True frugality is about understanding the connection, the dangerous link between things and my view of life, value, and others.

FRUGALITY AND MONEY

Richard Foster says, "Money is not something that is morally neutral, a resource to be used in good or bad ways, depending solely upon our attitude toward it."[2]

This is a bit too mystical and brooding for me, but his warning must be heeded. A rather more balanced view is that of John Wesley, who said, "Money is an excellent gift of God if it is used excellently, answering the noblest needs of humanity."[3] To Wesley, you see, money was not the enemy. The enemy is my own sinful nature. Therefore, in order to arrive at a balanced view of money, I must ask myself frugality's simple questions.

WHAT IS MONEY FOR?

Money is for exchange. Money is for goods and services that may, without corrupting my spirit, add education, comfort, and beauty to my life and to the lives of those I love. Furthermore, money is for the good of humanity and the expansion of God's kingdom. Money is never to be used for the purchase of status. Neither is it to be used for the demonstration of power.

WHO'S IN CHARGE HERE?

Am I controlling money, or is it controlling me? When ethical decisions are based on the bottom line of finances, money is in control. Are we making our decisions according to God or mammon? Man cannot serve two masters at one time. He will always love one and hate the other. Financial convenience corrupts faith and eats away at character, destroying submission to authority, humility, obedience, holiness, and patience.

Money must never control us. We must control it. I do not believe there is some mystical, evil power inherent in the dollar bill. What I do believe is that there is a weakness in my own flesh. Therefore I must humble myself under the hand of God. I must show mammon who is in charge here. It is the Lord Jesus Christ and not mammon.

WILL I LET CHARACTER SET THE LIMITS?

Am I willing for God to limit aspects of my life through a commitment to frugal living? In other words, when there is not enough money for me to pursue a certain course of action, am I willing to believe that it is not God's will for me to do it now? We confess that the abundance of funds can be used by God to affirm a course of action. If that is true, the contrary may also be true. From time to time God may pull tight the purse strings in order to stop me from a course that is not in His will. Therefore, lack of funds may be a way that

> CONSUMPTION WITHOUT FRUGALITY PRODUCES AN ESCALATING CYCLE OF THINGS WITHOUT PURPOSE.

God can use my commitment to frugal, modest living to keep me from continuing in a path that is wrong for me.

Frugality is the willingness to endure limits on myself. A serious danger inherent in the American credit system is that it allows me to consume at a level of superficial prosperity that is not based on any real wealth. We must again master the ancient art of waiting on things until we can pay for them. Credit can be a good thing, but its misuse destroys character. It creates an illusion of prosperity.

THE PLACE OF PROSPERITY

If I live a frugal life with a balanced view of money, what about prosperity in my life? I think the church has often failed to communicate a balanced view of prosperity. On the one hand, there are those who say money is altogether evil. Get it away from you. Give it away. Do not have anything to do with it. It is nasty and dirty and filthy, and it has a spirit in it that will get you. Then a need will arise to pay for something in the church, and they will ask folks to give money. Now, having told them how bad it is, they will ask God to give the congregation enough of it to support the church.

On the other hand, others say God is a God of riches. God wants to bless you, they reason, and if you are right with God, you are going to be rich. Therefore, if you are not rich, it must be because you are not right with God. Stranded between these two extremes are the majority of people who are living day-to-day on the money that they can earn while trying to provide for their families and improve their lives. What can we say to them?

John Wesley had a magnificent equation for this. He said to earn all you can. Earn it righteously. Earn it in a way that brings no shame to people and no shame to God. Earn all you can.

Second, save all you can. Now, saving all you can does not mean hoarding it. It means setting limits on my lifestyle in order that more might be made available to the kingdom of God and not go up in the smoke of mere spending. Saving all you can is crucial to frugality.

Earn all you can. Save all you can. Then Wesley adds the missing element: give all you can. Frugality saves to give. Greed gives to get. Frugality plots, plans, schemes, denies self, and sacrifices in order to give more next year than this year.

FREE TO BE FRUGAL

Frugality is the strength of character that will set us free from the terrible grip of mammon. It may not be immorality that finally erodes our national character. It may be the price of designer tennis shoes. The prosperity of God is a great blessing—a dangerous one, but a great one. If greatly used, prosperity can do much good. Hoarded or wasted, it corrupts character and destroys families. Oseola McCarty had it right. Work hard, serve folks joyfully, save frugally, and give generously.

> EARN ALL YOU CAN.
> SAVE ALL YOU CAN.
> GIVE ALL YOU CAN.

The toothless hag was terrifying to look at. Meega stared at the fearsome old woman and felt hot tears flood her eyes. The tears began to trace wet streaks down her smooth eleven-year-old cheeks. They dripped without being touched onto her bright native shirt. The chubby-faced little girl made no effort to hide or stem her tears. She did not even lift her little brown hands to wipe them away.

Her mother tried to comfort her, but what comfort could she give? Meega knew that the wretched-looking old creature was buying her from her father. The old buyer carefully counted baht into her father's eager palm. It was a great deal of money for a man as poor as her father.

Meega did not know what would happen to her in Bangkok. Other girls from her mountain tribe had been sold into the whorehouses. She knew that. She had heard the adults talk about it. What she did not know was exactly what a brothel was.

She was terrified and confused and hopeless. Sobs began to rack her body like the uncontrollable shakes of malaria. The old woman triumphantly laid the last baht into her father's outstretched hand. That hand quickly closed around the wrinkled, colored money *with a finality that made Meega scream.*

A few minutes later Meega's father watched as the woman walked briskly away down the winding jungle trail. At the end of a rope, following her like a lamb, walked his youngest daughter, her tiny hands bound behind her back. The old woman totally ignored the child's pitiable howls.

Now, the man said to himself, he could finally get that new radio he had wanted for so long. In fact, the stupid old witch had paid so much he could get a case of beer and some cigarettes and a lantern as well as the radio.

He watched the girl awhile longer, then turned back toward his hut. He fingered the roll of bills in the pocket of his shorts. Of course, he hated to see the girl go, but what is a girl compared to a radio?

VII

HONESTY—SUCCESS AND SELF-PRESERVATION

The best measure of a man's honesty isn't his income tax return. It's the zero adjust on his bathroom scale.

—Arthur C. Clarke

When the battleship *Ostfriesland* was sunk by bombs dropped from an American airplane, the career of General Billy Mitchell sank with it. The top brass in the post–World War I American army saw airplanes as expensive high-tech gadgets whose only purpose was battlefield reconnaissance. General Billy Mitchell, the commandant of the Army Air Corps in World War I, saw the future and dared to tell the truth. The next war, he said, would depend on air power. His counsel rejected, Mitchell arranged for a very public exhibition of that power. General Pershing and other World War I generals said it was impossible to sink a battleship from the air. It took Mitchell twenty minutes.

Mitchell's loyalty, foresight, genuine patriotism, and passion for the truth earned him a court-martial. Convicted of insubordination, branded a crackpot, and drummed out of the army he loved, Mitchell never backed down. He simply told the army and the country the truth.

Much of the nation and some in Congress listened, but the generals hated him and commanded him to be silent. He refused and continued lecturing and writing. In 1923, he was reduced in rank, and in 1925, despite a public outcry, he was court-martialed and suspended without pay.

The court-martial of General Billy Mitchell was an attempt to silence the truth, a truth that might have saved American lives and altered the course of history. His offense was telling the truth, and telling it with stunning accuracy. His analysis that Pearl Harbor was virtually defenseless to air attack from Japan was labeled as crazy and politically insensitive. His prediction that the Japanese would someday land paratroopers in Alaska was mocked and rejected as an attempt to gain support for an American paratroop corps that he advocated. Because rigid leadership rejected that truth, General Mitchell paid a heavy price for his honesty. Though a hero to some, he was a "renegade" to others, a rebel whose name was a joke in the highest levels of the military.

In 1936, he wrote, "All of the people who sat on my court-martial will be leading the forces defending our country in the Second World War. I hope someday they will be honest enough to admit they were wrong." He further wrote, "World War II will commence within five years." He died that same year with an estate worth a grand total of five thousand dollars. He lost everything because he told the truth. Mitchell did not live to see it, but the Japanese did bomb Pearl Harbor and did, in fact, land paratroopers in Alaska. World War II commenced within the five years he predicted, and the officers on his court-martial, including Douglas MacArthur, led the American forces.

In 1946, the army and the nation formally apologized to a man committed to tell the truth regardless of the cost. General

Billy Mitchell was posthumously awarded the Congressional Medal of Honor.[1]

One old proverb says, "As the twig is bent, so grows the tree." Habits, good or bad, cultivated early in life can determine success or failure later on. Cheating on an arithmetic quiz in fifth grade seems like a small issue, and slipping a candy bar in his pocket without paying by a junior high student may not be a Class A felony. Yet those are the very childish habits of cutting corners and "little white lies" that make for very grown-up failures. Learning early on to be honest with yourself and with others lies at the heart of true success.

In the early 1970s I ministered occasionally in the federal penitentiary in Atlanta. I have no idea whether I helped anyone on those visits, but I know they were a constant source of education for me.

One man I met there was named Eugene. He had embezzled hundreds of thousands of dollars from a corporation that sold infant products. Yet he complained bitterly that a country music artist had stolen a song he composed. Eugene made a clear distinction between "straightforward embez-zlement" and a "low-life thief who'd steal a man's song." His protestations were not of innocence but of honesty. He never claimed to be innocent. His bizarre reasoning was that he was honest about being dishonest. "I'm a thief," Eugene would say, "but at least I'm honest about it."

The really sobering thought, of course, is to consider the country music singer. How did he justify the theft to himself? "I'm no thief!" he surely tells himself. "I really have no idea where the original idea for that song came from. At least," he probably tells himself, "I never embezzled anything!"

Honesty is the virtue of wealth and words. Honesty in communication is telling the truth: "You shall not bear false witness against your neighbor" (Exod. 20:16). Honesty in possessions is right action with regard to things: "You shall not steal" (Exod. 20:15).

That is simple enough. The problem is that we are now living in a country that morally does not know its left hand from its right.

HONESTY AND POSSESSIONS

Hardly anyone argues in favor of theft. Even the thief objects when another thief steals his song. The problem, however, is to see honesty's subtle application to our lives. Many Americans see theft only as armed robbery. Anything short of that, they reason, is actually something else. Casual theft is a major financial and moral problem for America. The teenager who shoplifts, the thrill theft, the unpaid debt—these are the everyday thefts of America.

HONESTY IS THE VIRTUE OF WEALTH AND WORDS.

Faceless theft has become an acceptable crime. No one excuses robbing an old lady of her Social Security check, but to steal from an institution has become virtually heroic. It is different to steal from a company or a corporation, many people think.

Faceless theft starts with the wrong question. The question is not who or what owns a thing. The greater issue is who does not. Respect for private ownership transcends my ability to identify the owner. The fact that it is not mine is the bottom line. It is irrelevant that I do not know the rightful owner.

Prevailing "wisdom" claims that what I do *not* know is crucial to honesty. If I do not know whose it is, it may as well be mine. We must rearrange our thinking. Honesty must be based on what I do know. I may not know whose it is, but I certainly know whose it is not. Knowing it is not mine is the true ground of honesty. The point is not really that I have no right to what is yours. The point is, I have no right to that which is not mine.

HONEST GAIN

Honest financial improvement is an honorable goal. The selling of worthy goods or services for a fair price is pleasing in God's sight. There is nothing wrong with making a profit and gaining wealth. God wants His people to prosper.

However, the selling of goods for more than they are worth, even though the traffic will bear it, is dishonest. Willfully hiding information from another in order to get the better of him in a business deal is not shrewd business; it is robbery.

HONEST GAIN HONESTLY GOT

There is a line between shrewd business and dishonesty. However, it is not nearly as fine as we are led to believe. We would do far better to bend over backward for honesty. It is better to miss out on the deal than to make it by the slightest deception. It is better to make a minor profit with honesty than a major one without it.

Of course, honesty in selling is no less important than honesty in buying. Selling something for more than it is worth is dishonest, not clever. The used car lot that sells an automobile knowing that the transmission is on its last leg is operated by a band of thieves. The fact that they do not use guns is beside the point; they are still bandits.

Possessions are significant because they come from God. They are entrusted into our control. How we handle possessions, our own and those of others, is important. It is important because it is important to God.

HONESTY IN COMMUNICATION

Honesty is correct relationship with the highest level of reality. God Himself is ultimate reality. Truth is sacred because departure from truth is departure from God. The issue of truth is crucial to what we believe to be true about God and life.

Satan is a liar and the father of lies. Those who operate in right relationship to ultimate truth live in right relationship to who God is. They reflect the character of their Father. Those who deal in deception reveal who their true father is. Satan is the father of and the center of all deception in the earth.

There are two kinds of dishonest communication. The first is simulation; the second is dissimulation. *Simulation* is to seem to be what we are not. *Dissimulation* is to seem not to be what we are.

SIMULATION

Simulation includes all deceptive practices of image alteration. The craft of simulation includes such tools as exaggeration, make-believe, and hypocrisy. The image-conscious society in which we live hates truth and loves appearance.

An unspoken agreement of mutual deception rules the land. You pretend to believe my image, and I will pretend to accept yours. We both know it is not reality, and we both know the other knows it.

Yet we agree to the silent mutual deception because it suits us both.

Dissimulation

Dissimulation is appearing *not* to be what we really are. This is perhaps the more common crisis of faith for the average Western believer.

Most Christians will never be tempted to deny Christ before a firing squad. Few, relatively speaking, will be tortured to denounce His name. Far more often it is by silence or a head nod or a knowing wink that the modern believer denies his allegiance to Christ. The hypocrite pretends to be what he is not. The compromised, lacking the courage of their convictions, deny who they are.

> HONESTY IS CORRECT RELATIONSHIP WITH THE HIGHEST LEVEL OF REALITY.

"Let what you say be simply 'Yes' or 'No,'" the Bible says (Matt. 5:37). That may very well mean saying yes to Jesus when it is costly and no to the world when it is unpopular. The temptation will seldom be to outright denial but rather to minor compromises. Soft public denials are the coffin of bold and dynamic faith.

THE INSTINCT FOR DISHONESTY

The motivation for dishonesty is the instinct for self-preservation. The flesh says, "If I want it, I'll steal it. If I am not, I'll pretend to be. If I am, I'll pretend not to be. If I want to sell it, I will not tell everything." What can possibly shatter this powerful instinct?

Proverbs 22:4 says, "The reward for humility and fear of the LORD is riches and honor and life." Babies are not born with the fear of God. They are born with sin and an instinct for survival. Parents, governments, schools, and institutions are to instill the fear of God. If they fail in that duty, how will character ever be engraved upon young lives? In every human heart there is the thumbprint of the Creator. It is a homesickness for the image of God.

The closer a man lives to reality and truth, the more fully this inner longing is awakened. "You will know the truth, and the truth will set you free"

(John 8:32) is not simply a church slogan. It is the key to full humanity in the image of God.

Pontius Pilate, staring into the face of Jesus, asked his infamous question: "What is truth?"

Now listen to the answer of God: *I am the way, and the truth, and the life (John 14:6).*

Boynton's Mercedes turned off the main road. The gravel crunched under its wheels like tiny bones in the massive jaws of a great wolf. It was a good, powerful, masculine sound, and he liked it.

A bunny darted across the lane, and he could not resist the impulse to swerve the huge car. He did not hit the cottontail. He did not mean to hit it, but its frightened journey into the undergrowth made him chuckle. "That's one little rabbit with a traumatic tale of near death to share when it gets home."

As he drove, he enjoyed the peaceful scene spread out before him. The leaves on the massive oaks were in full fall plumage. The old gray fence posts and rusted barbed wire traced antique designs across the brown, overgrown fields. In fact, it was hard to believe he was only an hour and a half from downtown. Right here on this lonely gravel road he felt years away from the maddening crosstown connector and his own high-rise office building.

Only a few years before, these fields would have been full of cattle. Old lady Watson was not really farming any of this anymore. She had no family to help, and she lived all alone out here.

Why, he was doing her a favor. With the money

from this sale, she would be able to live comfortably until she died. Getting away from this farm was what she needed. She was lucky he came along. Anyone else might have really robbed her.

His cell phone rang just as the roof and twin chimneys of the Watson farmhouse nudged into view. As he answered, he noted the sagging roofline jutting above the soft, grassy-brown horizon.

"Hello," he answered.

"Hey, Boynton, it's Carl," the smooth voice of his partner responded. "Are you nearly there?"

"Yes," Boynton answered. "I can see the house from here. Your timing is perfect. What have you got for me? Is our information correct?"

"I checked with Commissioner Threllkell. It looks like the new loop is going right through the old Watson place. Have you got the check and the contract? Is she going to sign?"

"Calm down," Boynton reassured him. "It's in the bag. Are you sure your information is good?"

"I told you," Carl purred. "I talked to Threllkell himself. Of course, he wouldn't officially confirm the route."

"Of course." They both chuckled at the Threllkell joke. Threllkell was a fool, and they both knew it. Two weeks in the Bahamas every year assured Threllkell's unofficial dependability. "See you at the office in a few hours. Gotta go."

"Listen, Boynton, do you think the old lady has heard about the new loop yet?" Carl asked. The directness of the question irritated Boynton. Carl's lack of tact was a constant bother to Boynton.

"Don't be silly," he barked and hung up.

Boynton eased the metallic blue Mercedes to a halt in front of the charming old house with its wide-sweeping veranda. "It would be a real shame to knock this thing over," he thought. "A real shame." He stepped out of the Mercedes, stretched his arms over his head, and circled the car.

VIII

MEEKNESS—SUCCESS AND POWER

God bless thee; and put meekness in thy mind, love, charity,
obedience and true duty!

—William Shakespeare

Its young men done to death or in prisoner of war camps far in the north, its heartland in ashes, and its agriculture and industry destroyed, the South, in 1865, was shattered. Postwar poverty and a deep sense of shame and defeat gripped the states of the former Confederacy with economic and social depression.

The victorious North had not escaped the horrible Civil War without its own wounds. The rolls of the dead and wounded filled whole pages of the northern newspapers. Then, as reports of the violence in camps such as Andersonville became more public, the screams for revenge grew louder and more demanding. Many in power wanted the defeated South crushed and humiliated. The army and Congress wanted the conquered rebel states occupied, gutted, and forever stripped of full participation in the republic.

Abraham Lincoln, as war-weary as any, with as great a reason for vengeance as they, would have none of it. Whatever humiliating and malicious excesses were perpetrated during "reconstruction," none were Lincoln's fault. The South had rebelled, had cost the lives of thousands, and had devastated a generation for the sake of an unjust and immoral cause. Lincoln, with the power to punish them bitterly or even to return slavery for slavery, longed instead to return the wayward safely to the fold.

Abraham Lincoln, sixteenth president of the United States, had the South at his feet after Appomattox. His closest advisors, even his own cabinet, urged him to step on the throat of the defeated Confederacy and press down. Only his meekness, his refusal to use his power in unrestrained vengeance, saved the South and the nation from a postwar nightmare even worse than it was.

Lincoln, long known for his honesty, proved the depth of his great and noble character with meekness. In his second inaugural address, with the rebellious states of the Confederacy on their knees and the Union calling for revenge, Lincoln boldly called on Americans for healing love:

"With malice toward none; with charity for all; with firmness in the right, let us strive on to finish the work we are in; to bind up the nation's wounds; to care for him who shall have borne the battle, and for his widow, and his orphan—to do all which may achieve and cherish a just and lasting peace, among ourselves, and with all nations."[1]

Perhaps, even probably, you have never connected meekness and success. In fact, you only really need meekness when you are successful and powerful. Meekness is the virtue of the victor, not the defeated. Misunderstood by many, meekness is often thought to be only for weaklings. Nothing could be further from the truth. Meekness is the supreme virtue of leadership without which power becomes oppression. Meekness is power under control. Christianity itself is a contradiction that turns topside down the world's understanding of what it means to be successful.

Now in all virtues there is what might be called the conviction of the virtue. That is what we believe to be true about it. Then there is its theater of operation. That is, some circumstance is necessary to put the virtue in action. Fear, for example, must be present or courage cannot be called into action. In the same way, the rise to power calls for the virtue of meekness.

> MEEKNESS IS POWER UNDER CONTROL.

A big boy hits a small boy. The small boy endures it quietly because he has no other option. Inwardly, however, he longs for revenge. Because he is submissive in the face of violence, we may mislabel him as meek. Yet he is actually consumed with murderous rage. He forgoes vengeance, but he is not meek. He is simply resigned. If, however, the small boy hits the larger fellow, it is the offended party who has the power. He can break the smaller boy in half, yet he bears it quietly. That's meekness.

There are two words that taken together paint a completely wrong picture of meekness. Those two words are *meek* and *little*. We often say, "He is a meek little fellow." We envision this man as weak and powerless. In reality, however, we would be better to say, "What a big, strong, powerful, rugged meek fellow." When we identify meekness with being frail, we pervert the virtue.

Meekness is rarely provoked. It is easily calmed. It is controlled and patient. It is willing to forgive when forgiveness will earn no reward. Meekness is love in the driver's seat.

THE MEEKNESS OF JESUS CHRIST

Everything was spoken into existence, and nothing that we see was made without the Lord Jesus. Unto Him all things will return. It is appropriate for Him to consider Himself as having full rights in the Godhead. He is the second person of the Trinity! Yet, having full authority in the Godhead,

He laid all that aside and clothed Himself in mere mortality. Being found in the form of a man, He took upon Himself the likeness of a servant. (See Philippians 2:6–7.) (The word that is translated "servant" might even better be translated "slave.")

Therefore, Paul encourages us to own up to Christ's way of thinking. We are called to embrace His whole approach to living. Christ Jesus laid aside His rights as God to become not only a man but also a slave of men. Born in an occupied country under the authority of foreign soldiers, He was crucified by men whom He had created. God, willing to lay aside His authority over the earth and become earth, is meekness perfected.

THE BLESSINGS OF THE MEEK

There are great promises for the meek. Miss the virtue and miss the blessings.

CHRISTLIKENESS

Matthew 11:29 is an enlightening passage of Scripture: "Take my yoke upon you, and learn from me, for I am gentle and lowly in heart, and you will find rest for your souls."

We must settle ourselves into the double yoke with Jesus on one side and us on the other. The ox yoke thus securely around our necks, we learn His meekness. When He turns left, we turn left. When He turns right, we turn right. We learn to walk at His pace, to move when He moves and to stand still when He stops. When He pauses, we wait patiently. We fit ourselves to Jesus. We learn of Him; therefore, we learn about Him. The longer we walk with Him, the more we walk like Him. The longer we talk with Him, the more we talk like Him. His meekness becomes our meekness.

HAPPINESS

Meekness brings happiness in this life. Meekness makes a man fit to live with because he is not easily threatened by the loss of his power. Not constantly striving to gain control, the meek reject tactics of manipulation and intimidation.

Meekness likewise makes a man fit to do business with. Not needing to get the upper hand in every deal, the meek are to be trusted. Furthermore, because they are honest, the meek usually will prosper.

The meek will be happy in this life not only because they are fit to be with and fit to deal with, but also because they are able to be alone. A man who cannot stand to be alone with himself is a miserable person. A meek man, satisfied with the yoke of Jesus, is perfectly happy to be alone because he is, in fact, not alone. He who guides his footsteps also talks with him in the secret place.

INHERITANCE

The meek shall inherit the earth. *To inherit* means to come into authority, to gain dominion over. Matthew 5 may refer to the earth that God used to form our own "jars of clay" (2 Cor. 4:7). Self-possession, control over desires and passions, is the inheritance of the meek. The meek inherit—they have dominion over their own bodies.

There is also a future tense application to the promise. There *is* a new earth coming, an earth so beautiful and so perfect that it is not to be inherited by the greedy power-mongers of this age. This flawless new earth will be reserved only for the meek. After this earth is burned away along with its corrupt military, political, and economic power systems, the meek shall live and reign with Him eternally.

GUIDANCE

According to Psalm 25:9, God will guide the meek into what is right and teach them His way. Because of that, the meek live in peace instead of in the world's confusion and turmoil. The meek, submitted to the yoke of God and resting in His will, live without all the agonizing, gut-wrenching fear that grips the minds of the masses.

> THERE ARE GREAT PROMISES FOR THE MEEK. MISS THE VIRTUE AND MISS THE BLESSINGS.

JUDGMENT FOR MEEKNESS

God Himself, says Psalm 76:9, will judge and save all the meek of the earth. The meek can rest themselves in the face of injustices because ultimately God will set it right. I find that when we are the most outraged over injustice, we are most likely to lose touch with meekness. Meekness takes the patient, long-run view of God's justice.

There is something in us that longs to see the judgment of God visited on those that make terrorists and dictators into heroes. There is, however, a balance. We dare not turn a blind eye to injustices and become satisfied. However, justice and vengeance are not the same. God has ordained that on this earth civil government bears the sword for the purpose of rendering justice (Rom. 13:1–4). God can use the armies of the earth to punish the wicked, but the spirit of meekness will leave judgment to God. Vengeance and wrath are not emotions that humans are capable of handling. The reason God says, "Vengeance is mine," is not because vengeance is wrong. Vengeance is right. It must come, but it must never be in the wrong hands. We are inadequate to the task. Vengeance in our hands will destroy us. We are not God, and vengeance is a godly thing.

THE CHARACTER OF THE MEEK LEADER

The apostles asked, "Lord, who will be the greatest in Your kingdom?" For an answer Jesus took a basin of water, wrapped a towel around His waist, and began to wash their feet. Later when the might of Rome unleashed a holocaust against Christ's followers, that abiding memory of a meek Jesus willing to wash their feet gave them the power to topple an empire without drawing a sword.

There was an ancient and barbaric city that needed a new king. They called four of their leading citizens and said to each, "We're offering you the opportunity to be king of the city."

The key of the city was placed on a table before each man, one at a time.

The first was a warrior, a brave and courageous warrior whose victories in battle had won him great fame. They said, "Put both of your hands palm down on the table." The key of the city lay between them.

They said, "If you want to be king badly enough, you would be willing to lose one of your hands."

A man with an axe stood at the end of the table. "If you want the key, you may grasp it," said the people. "You can only move one of your hands, and the other one will be cut off. If you grasp the key with your right hand, the key is yours, and you will be the king, but you will lose your left."

The warrior wanted to be king more than anything else, so he reasoned within himself, "My right hand is my sword hand; I dare not lose it. My right hand is the source of my strength and power." Deciding to lose his left hand, he grabbed the key with his right hand.

Those barbaric citizens cruelly chopped off his left

hand and cast him out of the city. "Remnant, you are not worthy to be our king!"

The second was a philosopher. Not knowing the fate of the warrior, he struggled with the same question. They said to him, in turn, "Choose one." He reasoned within himself, "I write with my left hand, and the strength of my life is creativity. Therefore I will grasp the key with my left hand and let them chop off my right." The cruel city amputated the philosopher's right hand and cast him out of the city. "You are not worthy to be our king."

The third man was the richest merchant in the city. He did not know the fate of the other two. All he saw before him was the golden key and all the riches and power that it implied. His greed consumed him and, not thinking, he clutched the key with both hands. They cast him handless out of the city.

The fourth was a farmer. With the key between his hands, the question was put to him. He quickly withdrew both hands. The farmer explained, "My hands are my only means of service in this world. I will not sacrifice any of my ability to grow food for my fellow man merely for the sake of power." Instantly every citizen of the kingdom fell at his feet and crowned him king. They said, "Only one who despises power is worthy to have it."

IX

REVERENCE—SUCCESS AND VALUE

Reverence for life...does not allow the scholar to live for his science alone, even if he is very useful...the artist to exist only for his art, even if he gives inspiration to many.... It refuses to let the businessman imagine that he fulfills all legitimate demands in the course of his business activities. It demands from all that they should sacrifice a portion of their own lives for others.

—Dr. Albert Schweitzer

On Sunday you won't find any chicken or anything else to eat at any of Truett Cathy's 1,000-plus restaurants. Blasted by critics as legalistic, mocked by others for missing out on at least one-seventh of his potential revenue, yet amazingly successful, Cathy's quiet refusal to do business on Sunday remains unchanged.

The annual gross income of Chick-fil-A is estimated to be over $1 billion. That means that the company is missing out on at least $166 million annually. In fact, the amount lost is probably much more since Sunday, in most restaurants, is usually one of the best days, ironically enough, because of the after-church crowd. None of that will change Cathy's mind. He remains steadfast. Officials at Chick-fil-A are clear: "Admittedly, closing all of our restaurants every Sunday makes us a rarity in this day and age. But it's a little habit that has always served us well, so we're planning to stick with it."

When he launched his first restaurant in 1946, Truett Cathy made the decision to remain closed on Sundays. A loving, generous, and gracious man, Cathy never condemns those who do business or eat out on Sundays. His decision is his own, made out of his sense of reverence.

Cathy's was not a legalistic decision but one made out of respect for the things of God. In an age of casual disregard for things sacred, Cathy has earned the respect of even his harshest critics. A successful businessman and a generous donor, this giant of commerce is also a man of quiet reverence. Money or no money, the parking lot will be empty this Sunday at Truett Cathy's place.

Truett Cathy "wanted to ensure that every Chick-fil-A employee and restaurant operator had an opportunity to worship, spend time with family and friends, or just plain rest from the work week. Made sense then, still makes sense now."[1]

Success and failure are not so much matters of what we learn or earn or own. Success is measured and determined by what we reverence. As worth is assigned to things in a society, the individuals in it will carve out their legacy of success or failure.

If virtue is reverenced, virtue increases. If virtueless success or characterless talent is admired above all, character breaks down. A dangerous step toward collapse is taken when obvious irreverence is touted as a virtue.

Modern American humor is frighteningly irreverent. In the light of the whole counsel of God, we *must* recapture the serious reality that there are some things that are *not* to be made fun of. What is sacred to God must not be funny to us. Americans tend to say, "This movie was profane, wicked, horrible, murderous, and pornographic, but it was *so* funny," as though that excuses everything.

There are some things that *are* sacred, some things about which we simply should not make jokes. To jest of those things that are high and holy is to intrude dangerously on the things of God.

What is revered and how such reverence is demonstrated is important to a society's character. In other words, appropriate objects of reverence must be chosen and given their proper values. Then appropriate means of demonstrating that reverence must be found.

REVERENCE AND AWE

Our society has cultivated a deliberate boredom, a cynical resistance to being amazed, to wonder at anything. Many Americans spend their lives bored with everything and are themselves, therefore, monumentally boring. There are certain things that simply demand a response. It is arrogant and self-centered to stand for the first time at the foot of Mount Fuji and say, "Ho hum, it's about what I thought." How much more interesting life is with a person

> SUCCESS IS
> MEASURED AND
> DETERMINED
> BY WHAT WE
> REVERENCE.

who is unafraid to say, "I never dreamed it would be so beautiful!" There is something arrogant about a person who refuses to be impressed with anything. There are certain things in the presence of which I simply ought to be astonished.

Reverencing things outside myself takes my eyes off my own importance. When I develop the virtue of reverence, I cut away at my natural tendency to make myself the center of all things. The perspective that reverence returns to my life is not only spiritually important; it is also crucial to emotional well-being.

A contributing factor to the increasing madness of American culture is the decline of reverence. The loss of character in America, particularly the loss of reverence, is a subtle madness. Man, at the center of his own life, with all his problems and fears, unable to get his eyes off himself, is destined for emotional and spiritual collapse. Alone, man cannot stand the weight of himself.

ADMIRATION AND WORTHSHIP

To assign worth properly is *worth*ship. From this combination of words we get the single word *worship.* Character is weakened when worship is forsaken.

As individuals and societies assign worth, order priorities, and choose values, character is formed. "Worthship" ranges then from its lowest expression, mere respect, all the way to its highest, what I worship as God.

Admiration of particular individuals is one aspect of reverence. It is not wrong to admire certain qualities, abilities, or achievements of individuals. We must, however, be cautious not to admire wicked men.

> A CONTRIBUTING FACTOR TO THE INCREASING MADNESS OF AMERICAN CULTURE IS THE DECLINE OF REVERENCE.

Proverbs 17:15 says, "He who justifies the wicked and he who condemns the righteous are both alike an abomination to the LORD."

He who respects righteousness too lowly and he who respects unrighteousness too highly are an outrage to God. To idolize immoral actors, drug-addicted rock stars, and sports stars who are convicted criminals is to revere the unrighteous. We should show respect and admiration for achievements made in any field of endeavor, yet never forget that character remains the most important thing.

We must get right perspective to discern that which is worthy from that which is unworthy. We must see beyond popularity, past screaming crowds, more than mere wealth. Remember that he who honors the dishonorable and he who respects the righteous too lowly are both an abomination to God.

REVERENCE AND SEX

Reverence for sex is a deeply confused issue. Even among those opposed to pornography and prostitution there are many who do not understand why these are evil. Pornography does not make sex more important than God. That is a common misconception about the "philosophy" of pornography. That is not what pornography is about. Pornography makes sex so low and common that we may treat it any way we want. Pornography is based on the premise that sex is unimportant. The reason pornography is wrong is not because sex is wrong. The reason pornography is wrong is because it makes sex too unimportant. Pornography does not reverence sex. The Bible does. Sex is important because it was made by God. Hugh Hefner did not invent sex. God invented sex. Sex is a good thing, a holy thing, not to be used without the reverence it deserves.

REVERENCE AND LIFE

We must reverence life itself. The reason abortion is wrong is because human life is the creation of God. To do away with life selfishly because we have our own view of worth is wrong. Life must be valued over convenience, over finances, over reputation, and over relationships. Life is holy because God made life. When self-interest is worth more than life, character gives way to madness.

> WE MUST GET RIGHT PERSPECTIVE TO DISCERN THAT WHICH IS WORTHY FROM THAT WHICH IS UNWORTHY.

When men and nations drift into irreverence, their very reason for living is lost. Ultimately, insanity awaits when character loses reverence. When I know God is ultimately worthy, my sense of worthship is restored. When my sense of worthship is restored, my longing to worship comes again. If society assigns ultimate worth to anything except God Himself, reverence turns to madness and madness to despair. The Bible is perfectly clear. This world and the sky that we see will burn with fire. If I reverence that which will disappear, I make myself temporary. If I place my reverence in Jesus, then my perspective and my future are eternal.

The Cossacks, more bored than angry, sat on their horses and stared at the sky, muttering to themselves that snow—probably lots of snow—was on its way. They were warriors, made for battles. They were not policeman for herding Jews like cattle. The czar wanted this Jewish community moved, and they would move them, but it was boring, cold work; they would not pretend to like it.

"You, there," Sergeant Ivanovich barked. "Hurry it up. That will not break, you know. Just throw it on the cart and get on with it."

"No," the old rabbi answered, "it will not break. It can be broken, but it will not break."

Sergeant Ivanovich snorted and shrugged. Why did the czar hate these Jews? Ivanovich could not understand it. Then again, he could not understand the Jews either. It can be broken but it will not break. What nonsense.

"I don't have time for riddles, you old fool. Just toss it up there."

Ignoring him, the rabbi continued, without hurrying, to wrap carefully the long-handled rolls as if they were made of crystal. If the old man was frightened of Ivanovich, it was not noticeable. What was noticeable was that whatever was in the odd, tubelike rolls was precious to the rabbi.

"What have you got there anyway?" Ivanovich demanded.

"The Torah."

"What?"

"The Torah," the old man repeated, looking for the first time at the young sergeant. "Do you know what that means... Torah?"

"Is it valuable?"

"No, not as you mean valuable. You could not get much for this ragged old scroll. It determines the value of all else, but it is of little value itself. There, I'm finished."

"Good, toss it up there and get your people moving."

"I will carry it," the rabbi said.

"For three hundred miles?"

"It has carried me for seventy-eight years and my people before me for thousands of years. I can carry it for a few hundred miles."

Ivanovich shrugged, "Suit yourself."

"Never," the rabbi muttered, but Ivanovich pretended not to hear. Instead he spun his horse and charged back down the column of carts filled with the *few possessions the Jews owned. The burly sergeant knew in his heart that the czar had made a mistake. There was no use persecuting people like this, people who, owning nothing of value, would carry a tattered scroll as if it were pure gold.*

X

GRATITUDE—SUCCESS AND HUMILITY

Gratitude is merely the secret
hope of further favors.

—FRANÇOIS DE LA ROCHEFOUCAULD

Her evangelistic ministry was just beginning to take off when Kathryn Kuhlman was blindsided by what might have derailed her. Though separated for years from her first husband, she was not seeking a divorce. When he sued for divorce in Arizona, she was in an extended and powerfully anointed crusade in Franklin, Ohio. If word of the divorce had hit the front page, she would have been finished. In 1948, a divorced female evangelist was not possible.

The papers were served on her by the county sheriff personally. She was devastated. Her past had erupted into her present with the power to destroy her future. With a trembling hand she received the papers from the sheriff, but when she looked into his eyes, Kuhlman was shocked to find tender mercy.

"My office ordinarily releases the names of all divorces to the local newspaper," he explained. "But I have been attending your services, and I am convinced God sent you to this crime-riddled county for a special purpose. There is no need for anyone but the two of us to know what has happened. God bless you and your ministry among us. I am at your service."

The young female preacher was overcome with gratitude. She told the police officer, "I will be grateful to you for the rest of my life."

Seven years later when the "news" of her divorce finally broke in the Akron newspaper, it was old news and her ministry was far too strong for the story to do much damage. The sheriff had given her the time she needed, and she never forgot him.

Every year, until the day of his death nearly a quarter of a century later, that burly sheriff received an expensive flower arrangement on his birthday. The card always said the same thing, "With gratitude from Kathryn Kuhlman."[1]

If you want to be remembered by those you meet, if you want to be admired by colleagues and praised by your friends, then be grateful. Gratitude is a key to success simply because it is so rare as to be remembered. The kid who can hit jump shots may be a star today but a nobody tomorrow. However, the kid who returns to say thank you to the businessman who gave him money to buy a basketball—that kid is a success his whole life.

Some years ago I was counseling with a teenager who had been raised from infancy by his grandparents. The boy's father had been killed in an automobile accident, and subsequently his mother disappeared. The grandparents had been doing all they could for him at great expense to themselves. It is difficult for anyone to raise a teenager, and people in their sixties and seventies ought not to have to go through it a second time around.

For several years he rewarded them with rebellion, anger, and sin until he made his grandparents miserable. I told him, "They did not have to take you in. You could have gone to an orphanage. You could have been a ward of the court. They got up with you in the middle of the night. They changed your diapers and fed you and clothed you. They raised you at great sacrifice to themselves. Nobody would have blamed them if they had said, 'We just can't handle it at our age.'"

He replied bitterly, "Do you think this is the first time I've ever thought of all that? I know what they've done. What am I supposed to do, spend the rest of my life saying 'thank you'?"

Well, yes! A thousand times *yes*! You're supposed to spend the rest of your life saying "thank you." Everyone is. That is what real life is—an expression of gratitude to God. *Yes*, we are supposed to spend the rest of our lives, every waking moment, saying "thank you." That is what the apostle Paul said. "I consider myself to be in debt, both to the Greek and to the non-Greek. I am indebted to the whole world. I am in debt to *God*!" (See Romans 1:14.)

The reason we resist the life of never-ending gratitude is fear that "thank you" means responsibility. What the corrupt character wants is to be free from the responsibility to, in any way, "pay some of it back." The great tragedy of many Americans is their ingratitude. Somehow they believe they deserve it all.

A Sin of the Rich

Ingratitude is, in general, not a sin of the poor but of the rich, and we are rich. Look at us. A kid who has never had anything and has no hope of having anything, who wakes up cold every morning of his life in a tiny shack, is likely to be grateful for the apple he gets at Christmas. The kid who wakes up every morning in a $350,000 house and who has never worked a day in his life, who puts hundreds of dollars' worth of clothes on his well-scrubbed back every morning and is driven to a private school (that somebody else is paying for), complains about the laptop he gets for Christmas because it does not have all the software he wanted.

Ingratitude, a curse to everyone it touches, is a habit that destroys character. The child taken for ice cream complains because there are no chocolate sprinkles on top. Nothing is ever quite right. Nothing is ever quite enough. Parents save and sacrifice to take their children to Disney World, and the children think that somehow they deserve it. It seldom occurs to them that, out of their love for them, their parents are spending, perhaps, the worst week of their entire lives. Even less frequently does it occur to American children this is something for which they actually ought to be grateful.

Parents pay for expensive tickets to a theme park, fork over eight dollars for a hot dog that tastes like sawdust, and go on rides that make them wish they were dead. At the end of the day the parents, exhausted and dead broke, want only to know that their children are happy and grateful. The well-developed character says, "This is more than I deserve. This is perfect." Not, "This will do." Not, "OK, I guess." But, "Thanks! This is perfect, and I do *not* deserve perfect."

> THE GREAT TRAGEDY OF MANY AMERICANS IS THEIR INGRATITUDE. SOMEHOW THEY BELIEVE THEY DESERVE IT ALL.

Ingratitude is actually a form of selfishness, and it can be devastating to the feelings of others. Children, do not face the day that your mother says, "Daddy isn't coming home from work. Something terrible happened at the office," only to realize that you never said, "Thanks, Dad."

There are American teens who would rather stay home from school than show up in tennis shoes from the neighborhood discount store. Life's critical issue in America has become the brand name on our tennis shoes. In Rwanda today, there are teens who pray, "O God, just once before I die, could I wear a pair of shoes? Any kind of shoes?"

This is not to pile on guilt. It is rather to say that we must awaken to the reality that we are in debt. We are the richest, most powerful, most prosperous, most educated, cleanest, healthiest people who have ever been on the face of the earth. Instead of being the most grateful, we are often the most selfish, self-centered, ungrateful people who have ever lived.

HABITUAL GRATITUDE

All ingratitude is basically ingratitude to God. God blesses us with health and happiness, but we sulk because we are not the president of the United States. We pray for a job, and when we get one, we whine about the pay. A woman prays for a new house and resents having to clean it. A single woman prays to get married and then lives in angry depression because her long-awaited husband is not perfect.

151

We are seldom just grateful to God. God gives us the strawberry sundae, and we complain because it doesn't have whipped cream. He gives us the whipped cream, and we moan for a cherry on top. At some point we must say, "It is *enough*. I am content with this. It is more than I deserve."

Gratitude as well as ingratitude can become a habit of life. We can begin to see everything that happens to us as an opportunity to praise God. Gratitude can be added to character.

> GRATITUDE AS WELL AS INGRATITUDE CAN BECOME A HABIT OF LIFE.

We must get specific with God. Instead of complaining about having to wear this or that kind of shirt, thank God you have a shirt. Gratitude is a learned way of life. It is the open hand instead of the clenched fist. It is saying "yours" and not "mine." It is the Spirit of Jesus and not the spirit of the world.

Character is not built by just mindlessly obeying the rules. It is learned best by celebrating the joy of God's grace. Character lived or taught in a rules-oriented method destroys joy. The celebration of character development is not an oppressive duty. There is joy and meaning to be found in serving God, who has given us more than we could ever pay back. The character to live in gratitude is the key to success.

———— ⌘ ————

A mighty raja in ancient India had a gardener who was a constant thief. The nobleman overlooked it for years because the gardener never stole anything very precious. Finally, however, the man stole one of the crown jewels. After prying a ruby of enormous value out of the royal crown, the wicked gardener fled in the night on a horse stolen from the stable. In the dark, as he rode the nobleman's horse wildly out of the royal compound, he trampled the nobleman's son and killed him.

Some days later the raja's soldiers captured the murderous thief and dragged him before the raja. With the executioner's broadsword poised over his neck, the apologetic thief cried, "Please, mighty master, have mercy on me. Don't kill me—if not for my sake, then for the sake of my wife and five children. I plead, don't kill me."

The great and gracious raja forgave him. He forgave him not only the thievery but also the death of his son. He even reinstated him as gardener. Yet, three months later the gardener was again hurled before the raja. He had stolen a nearly worthless cup from the royal kitchen.

The great raja said, "Bring the swordsman and cut his head off. Execute him here in my presence."

The gardener did not dare to plead for his life. Instead he said, "I deserve to die. But I don't understand. You forgave me for the death of your son. Will you now execute me for the theft of a kitchen utensil?"

The raja said, "No, you really don't understand. I'm not executing you for the theft of a cup. I'm executing you for the sin of ingratitude."

Notes

Chapter 2
Courage—the Key to the Keys of Success

1. Jeordan Legon, "Soldier Risks Life to Rescue Civilian Caught in the Crossfire," Heroes of War, CNN.com, http://www.cnn.com/SPECIALS/2003/iraq/heroes/carter.html (accessed September 12, 2007).

Chapter 3
Loyalty—Success in Relationships

1. Sam Houston Memorial Museum, "Chronology of Sam Houston's Life," http://www.shsu.edu/~smm_www/History/ (accessed September 12, 2007); and, Sam Houston Memorial Museum, "Notable Quotes of Sam Houston," http://www.shsu.edu/~smm_www/History/quotes.shtml (accessed September 12, 2007).

CHAPTER 4
DILIGENCE—SUCCESS IN WORK

1. GaleGroup.com, "Black History: George Washington Carver," http://www.galegroup .com/free_resources/bhm/bio/carver_g.htm (accessed October 30, 2007).

CHAPTER 5
MODESTY—SUCCESS AND SIMPLICITY

1. Author's personal observations and personal research on James Blanchard.

CHAPTER 6
FRUGALITY—SUCCESS AND PROSPERITY

1. Sharon Wertz, "Oseola McCarty Donates $150,000 to Southern Miss," University of Southern Mississippi press release, June 26, 1995, http://www.usm.edu/pr/oola1.htm (accessed October 31, 2007).

2. Richard Foster, *Money, Sex and Power* (San Francisco: Harper and Row, 1985).

3. John Wesley, "The Use of Money," *The Collected Works of John Wesley* (Chicago: Baker House, n.d.).

CHAPTER 7
HONESTY—SUCCESS AND SELF-PRESERVATION

1. HomeoftheHeroes.com, "Wings of Valor—
   The Battle at Home and the Court-Martial
   of Billy Mitchell," http://www
   .homeofheroes.com/wings/part1/6_
   survival.html (accessed November 1, 2007).

CHAPTER 8
MEEKNESS—SUCCESS AND POWER

1. The Avalon Project at Yale Law School,
   "Second Inaugural Address of Abraham
   Lincoln," Saturday, March 4, 1865, http://
   www.yale.edu/lawweb/avalon/presiden/
   inaug/lincoln2.htm (accessed November 2,
   2007).

CHAPTER 9
REVERENCE—SUCCESS AND VALUE

1. Chick-fil-A.com, "Closed Sundays. It's Part
   of the Chick-fil-A Recipe," http://www
   .chick-fil-a.com/Closed.asp (accessed
   November 2, 2007); "We're Here to Serve.
   And Not Just Sandwiches," http://www
   .chick-fil-a.com/Company.asp (accessed
   November 2, 2007); "Company Fact Sheet,"
   http://www.chick-fil-a.com/FactSheet.asp
   (accessed November 2, 2007).

Chapter 10
Gratitude—Success and Humility

1. Jamie Buckingham, *Daughter of Destiny: Kathryn Kuhlman...Her Story* (Plainfield, NJ: Logos International, 1976), 112–113.

OTHER BOOKS BY MARK RUTLAND

Launch Out Into the Deep

Behind the Glittering Mask

Streams of Mercy

God of the Valleys

Nevertheless

Dream

Power

Holiness

Resurrection

Character Matters

For more information about Global Servants
or to receive a product list
of the many books, CDs, and DVDs
by Mark Rutland,
write, call, or go online:

Global Servants
1601 Williamsburg Square
Lakeland, FL 33803
Toll free: (888) 823-8772
www.globalservants.org

For more information about
Oral Roberts University write, call, or go online:

Oral Roberts University
7777 South Lewis Avenue
Tulsa, Oklahoma 74171
(800) 678-8876 (Main Number)
www.oru.edu

W e hope that the life-changing words shared by Dr. Mark Rutland will encourage you as you follow your dreams to success.

Here are two more books by Dr. Rutland that will continue to help you grow into the life God has for you!

Nevertheless

With one unassuming word, Jesus freed us and revealed the love of God. In the Garden of Gethsemane, one word saved a race that deserved no saving; "*nevertheless*," Jesus prayed, and heaven and earth rejoiced.

978-0-88419-847-5 / $9.99

Dream

God has great plans for your life but His dreams for you are even bigger! Reach out and touch your dreams, look at them, and hold on to them tightly, but above all else... dare to dream!

978-0-88419-890-1 / $9.99

Available where fine Christian books are sold.

Charisma
H O U S E
A STRANG COMPANY 7732